Introduction to Distributed Self-Stabilizing Algorithms

Synthesis Lectures on Distributed Computing Theory

Editor
Michel Raynal, *University of Rennes, France and Hong Kong Polytechnic University*

Synthesis Lectures on Distributed Computing Theory is edited by Michel Raynal of the University of Rennes, France and Nancy Lynch of the Massachusetts Institute of Technology. The series publishes 50- to 150-page publications on topics pertaining to distributed computing theory. The scope largely follows the purview of premier information and computer science conferences, such as ACM PODC, DISC, SPAA, OPODIS, CONCUR, DialM-POMC, ICDCS, SODA, Sirocco, SSS, and related conferences. Potential topics include, but not are limited to: distributed algorithms and lower bounds, algorithm design methods, formal modeling and verification of distributed algorithms, and concurrent data structures.

Introduction to Distributed Self-Stabilizing Algorithms

Karine Altisen, Stéphane Devismes, Swan Dubois, and Franck Petit

ISBN: 978-3-031-00885-6   paperback
ISBN: 978-3-031-02013-1   eBook
ISBN: 978-3-031-00131-4   hardcover

DOI 10.1007/978-3-031-02013-1

A Publication in the Springer series
SYNTHESIS LECTURES ON DISTRIBUTED COMPUTING THEORY

Lecture #15
Series Editor: Michel Raynal, *University of Rennes, France and Hong Kong Polytechnic University*
Founding Editor: Nancy Lynch, *Massachusetts Institute of Technology*
Series ISSN
Print 2155-1626   Electronic 2155-1634

Introduction to Distributed Self-Stabilizing Algorithms

Karine Altisen
VERIMAG/Grenoble INP, Grenoble, France

Stéphane Devismes
VERIMAG/Université de Grenoble Alpes, Grenoble, France

Swan Dubois
LIP6/Sorbonne Université, Paris, France

Franck Petit
LIP6/Sorbonne Université, Paris, France

SYNTHESIS LECTURES ON DISTRIBUTED COMPUTING THEORY #15

ABSTRACT

This book aims at being a comprehensive and pedagogical introduction to the concept of *self-stabilization*, introduced by Edsger Wybe Dijkstra in 1973 [Dij73]. Self-stabilization characterizes the ability of a distributed algorithm to converge within finite time to a configuration from which its behavior is correct (i.e., satisfies a given specification), regardless the arbitrary initial configuration of the system. This arbitrary initial configuration may be the result of the occurrence of a finite number of transient faults. Hence, self-stabilization is actually considered as a versatile non-masking fault tolerance approach, since it recovers from the effect of any finite number of such faults in an unified manner. Another major interest of such an automatic recovery method comes from the difficulty of resetting malfunctioning devices in a large-scale (and so, geographically spread) distributed system (e.g., the Internet, Pair-to-Pair networks, and Delay Tolerant Networks are examples of such distributed systems). Furthermore, self-stabilization is usually recognized as a lightweight property to achieve fault tolerance as compared to other classical fault tolerance approaches. Indeed, the overhead, both in terms of time and space, of state-of-the-art self-stabilizing algorithms is commonly small. This makes self-stabilization very attractive for distributed systems equipped of processes with low computational and memory capabilities, such as wireless sensor networks.

After more than 40 years of existence, self-stabilization is now sufficiently established as an important field of research in theoretical distributed computing to justify its teaching in advanced research-oriented graduate courses. This book is an initiation course, which consists of the formal definition of self-stabilization and its related concepts, followed by a deep review and study of classical (simple) algorithms, commonly used proof schemes and design patterns, as well as premium results issued from the self-stabilizing community. As often happens in the self-stabilizing area, in this book we focus on the proof of correctness and the analytical complexity of the studied distributed self-stabilizing algorithms.

Finally, we underline that most of the algorithms studied in this book are actually dedicated to the high-level *atomic-state* model, which is the most commonly used computational model in the self-stabilizing area. However, in the last chapter, we present general techniques to achieve self-stabilization in the low-level message passing model, as well as example algorithms.

KEYWORDS

distributed computing, distributed algorithms, fault tolerance, transient faults, self-stabilization, convergence, closure, stabilization time, atomic-state model, daemons

Out of chaos, stars are born.

Charlie Chaplin

Contents

Preface

Why this book? In 1974, Edsger Wybe Dijkstra publishes his seminal work on *self-stabilization*, with relative anonymity, as a two-page paper in the international journal *Communications of the ACM* (Association for Computing Machinery) [Dij74].[1] This small-length article is then remained almost unknown by the distributed computing community until being highlighted by Leslie Lamport in an invited talk at the international conference PODC 1983 (ACM Symposium on Principles of Distributed Computing) [Lam85]. Leslie Lamport pointed out the importance of this work, especially the elegance of the concept of self-stabilization as a general approach for fault tolerance. Precisely, he stated the following now famous quote.

> "*I regard this as Dijkstra's most brilliant work – at least, his most brilliant published paper. It's almost completely unknown. I regard it to be a milestone in work on fault tolerance. [...] I regard self-stabilization to be a very important concept in fault tolerance and to be a very fertile field for research.*"

As a matter of fact, the Dijkstra's paper [Dij74] received the 2002 ACM PODC Influential-Paper Award, one of the highest recognitions in the distributed computing community. Moreover, after Dijkstra's death, the award was renamed and is now called the Dijkstra Award.

In 1983, the research community on self-stabilization was born and, since then, never stopped growing. A biennial international workshop called WSS (Workshop of Self-Stabilization) was created in 1989 to gather the community. This workshop became the annual international conference SSS (conference on Stabilization, Safety, and Security) in 2003, and still exists today.

After more than 40 years of intensive research, self-stabilization is now an unavoidable topic in the main distributed computing conferences, such as PODC and DISC (Symposium on DIStributed Computing). Moreover, although being exclusively an academic field at the beginning, self-stabilization now finds applications in real daily-life networking protocols [DOTF94]. Furthermore, self-stabilizing version of classical routing protocols, such as BGP (Border Gateway Protocol), the standard inter-domain routing protocol in the Internet, has been proposed [CDT05].

Self-stabilization is now taught in the research master's degree of many prestigious university, e.g., TU Berlin (Germany), Sorbonne Université (France), ETH Zürich (Switzerland), Chalmers University (Sweden), the University of Texas at Austin (USA), MIT (USA), Ohio State University (USA), to quote only a few.

---

[1]This paper is actually based on a technical report written in 1973 [Dij73].

Content.   In this book, we present basic principles and classical techniques used to design, prove, and analyze distributed self-stabilizing algorithms. In an educational and awareness large-scale concern, we focus on algorithms written in the (high-level) *atomic-state* model introduced by E. W. Dijkstra in his seminal paper [Dij74]. The atomic-state model is the most commonly used computational model in the self-stabilizing community. However, notice that the last chapter reviews basic techniques to design self-stabilizing algorithms in the (low-level) message passing model.

Actually, few books of the distributed computing literature, e.g., [Tel01, Gho14, Dol00], present the self-stabilizing paradigm. Notably, until now, the book of Shlomi Dolev [Dol00] was the only one to be fully dedicated to self-stabilization. This latter is an exhaustive survey that broadly covers the existing literature. Here, we adopt the opposite approach by focusing on a few number of fundamental algorithms. However, those algorithms are representative of the main problems explored so far in the field: from local (e.g., node coloring) to global (e.g., Breadth-First Search spanning tree) and from static (e.g., Breadth-First Search spanning tree) to dynamic (e.g., token circulation) tasks. Reducing the scope allowed us to extensively investigate the presented algorithms. As a matter of fact, each chapter is built according to the following didactic guideline. Although simple, the problems and their solution are deeply studied. Proofs of self-stabilization are investigated in detail and illustrated with pedagogical examples. Finally, a particular focus is made on the tightness of both parameters and complexity bounds. In more detail, the book begins with a large introduction where, in particular, advantages, drawbacks, and limits of self-stabilization are discussed. The atomic-state model is exhaustively presented in the next chapter. The four following chapters are dedicated to the deep investigation of particular (well-known) self-stabilizing algorithms written in the atomic-state model. These chapters are organized with respect to an increasing level of difficulty. Before the last chapter about self-stabilization in message passing, a chapter is dedicated to the notion of composition, which is central in self-stabilization to allow the design of more complex distributed self-stabilizing solutions.

Audience.   This book has been written primarily for teachers who want to prepare a lecture on self-stabilization, or include self-stabilization in their teaching on distributed systems, and in particular, in lessons dealing with fault tolerance. For example, using this book, foundations of self-stabilization can be presented in a master-class right after an introductory course on distributed algorithms.

This book also targets graduate and Ph.D. students in computer science or computer engineering who are interested in distributed algorithms in general. Prerequisites for this book include discrete mathematics, set theory, graph theory, first-order logic, and algorithmic. Basic knowledges on distributed algorithms would be valuable, but are not mandatory.

Karine Altisen, Stéphane Devismes, Swan Dubois, and Franck Petit
April 2019

Acknowledgments

The authors are very grateful to Professor Michel Raynal for inviting them to publish this book. We would like also to thank Doctor Erwan Jahier, Professor Sandeep Kulkarni, and Professor Toshimitsu Masuzawa for their meticulous review of this book and their valuable suggestions.

We are especially thankful to our co-author, mentor, and faithful friend, Ajoy Kumar Datta, Professor at University of Las Vegas Nevada. Since 1995, Ajoy K. Datta has greatly contributed to the development of WSS (Workshop of Self-Stabilization) that became an annual international Symposium thereafter. Without Ajoy K. Datta, self-stabilization would probably not have the recognition it has today.

We address a very special dedication to Joffroy Beauquier, Sylvie Delaët, and Colette Johnen who widely participated to the introduction of self-stabilization in France and more widely, in Europe. Including Vincent Villain, these four researchers are undoubtedly behind our enthusiasm for self-stabilization.

Finally, we would like to thank our friends, colleagues, and co-authors that helped us a lot along the years in contributing to the self-stabilizing field.

Karine Altisen, Stéphane Devismes, Swan Dubois, and Franck Petit
April 2019

CHAPTER 1

Introduction

1.1 PARABLE OF THE COLLATZ CONJECTURE

Assign an arbitrary positive integer value to a variable u and apply the following (sequential) algorithm, noted A in the sequel:

1: **while** true **do**
2:    print u
3:    **if** u is even **then**
4:       $u \leftarrow \frac{u}{2}$
5:    **else**
6:       $u \leftarrow 3 \times u + 1$
7:    **end if**
8: **end while**

For example, initializing u to 12, we obtain the infinite sequence:

$$s = 12, 6, 3, 10, 5, 16, 8, 4, 2, 1, 4, 2, 1 \ldots$$

Remark that s is composed of a finite prefix followed by the infinite repeating suffix $(4, 2, 1)^{\omega}$. Try another initial value, say 29. We obtain the following infinite sequence:

$$s' = 29, 88, 44, 22, 11, 34, 17, 52, 26, 13, 40, 20, 10, 5, 16, 8, 4, 2, 1, 4, 2, 1 \ldots$$

Again, $(4, 2, 1)^{\omega}$ is an infinite suffix of s'.

Actually, until now, such a convergence phenomenon has been observed for every tested initial (positive integer) value. But, there is still no proof showing the ineluctable convergence of the process regardless of which positive integer is chosen initially: this open problem is known as the *Collatz conjecture* (or *Syracuse problem*).

Define the current configuration of A to be the value of variable u. So, the set of all possible configurations of A is $\mathbb{N}^*$. Divide the possible configurations of A into two sets: the set of *legitimate configurations* $\{1, 2, 4\}$ and the set of *illegitimate configurations* $\mathbb{N}^* \setminus \{1, 2, 4\}$; see the Venn diagram in Figure 1.1.

Then, the Collatz conjecture can be reformulated as follows:

Is Algorithm A self-stabilizing?

Indeed, intuitively, a *self-stabilizing* algorithm, regardless of its initial configuration, reaches within finite time a legitimate configuration (*Convergence* property) and remains in the legitimate set of configurations thereafter (*Closure* property) [Dij73, Dij74].

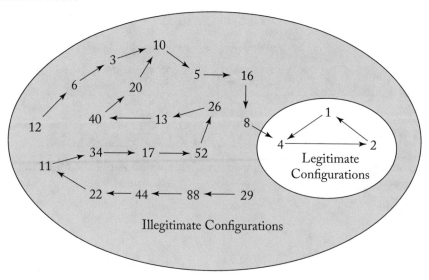

Figure 1.1: Configurations of A.

1.2   DISTRIBUTED SELF-STABILIZING SYSTEMS

The concept of *self-stabilization* was introduced by Dijkstra in 1973 [Dij73] in the context of distributed systems, i.e., systems made of a finite set of autonomous processes interconnected through a communication network, which aim at accomplishing a global objective. In this case, the design of (distributed) self-stabilizing algorithms may seem to be quite intricate since each computing entity, i.e., process, has to coordinate with each other despite it has only a partial view of the system: its local state and information transmitted through, usually *asynchronous*, communication media linking the process to a part of the other processes. However, it is worth noticing that, like the examples studied in this book, numerous distributed self-stabilizing algorithms are, perhaps surprisingly, elegant and even sometimes simpler than their non-stabilizing counterpart [Tel01].

1.2.1   MAJOR ADVANTAGE: FAULT TOLERANCE

The main interest of self-stabilization lies in enabling the design of distributed systems tolerating *any finite* number of *transient faults*. A transient fault occurs at an unpredictable time, but does not result in a permanent hardware damage. Moreover, as opposed to intermittent faults, the frequency of transient faults is considered to be low. Consequently, network components (processes or links) affected by transient faults temporarily deviate from their specifications, e.g., some bits in a process local memory can be flipped, some messages in a link may be lost, reordered, duplicated, or even corrupted. As a result, a transient fault affects the state of the component in which it occurs. Hence, after a finite number of transient faults, the configuration of a distributed system may be arbitrary, i.e., variables in process memories may have arbitrary values taken in their respective definition domains (e.g., a Boolean variable is either true or false) and communication links may contain a finite number of correctly formatted but arbitrary valued messages (n.b., it is commonly assumed that any message is still correctly formatted after transient faults, since otherwise the message can be simply discarded). However, the time before the next transient perturbation is long enough to allow the system to eventually resume a correct behavior; see Figure 1.2.

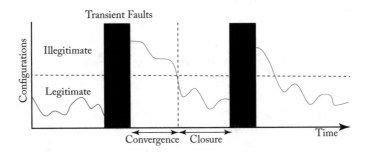

Figure 1.2: Fault tolerance of self-stabilizing systems.

In contrast with most of existing fault tolerance approaches (a.k.a., robust approaches), self-stabilization is a non-masking method: it does not hide the effect of the faults, authorizing the system to (temporarily) deviate from its specification, i.e., the formal definition of the problem it should solve. As a result, the faults are not directly treated, rather their consequences. Moreover, convergence is only guaranteed if there is a sufficiently large time window without any fault. Hence, *in the proof of correctness*, the initial point of observation is after the occurrence of the "last" faults and there is no fault model in the literal sense. That is, the system is studied starting from an arbitrary configuration reached due to the occurrence of some transient faults, but from which it is assumed that *no fault will ever occur*; see Figure 1.3. By abuse of language, this configuration is referred to as the *initial configuration* of the system in the literature. Then, starting from an arbitrary initial configuration, an algorithm is self-stabilizing if it guarantees that the system automatically (i.e., without any external, e.g., human, intervention) converges *within finite time* to a closed set of so-called legitimate configurations from which every possible suffix of execution is correct, i.e., satisfies the *specification* of the considered problem. Notice that this definition implicitly assumes that faults do not alter the code of the algorithm. This assumption is justified in [Dol00] by the following two arguments. The code of a self-stabilizing algorithm can be hardwired in a ROM (Read Only Memory) which cannot be corrupted. Another solution consists of saving a duplication of the code in trusted long-term memory, such as an hard disk, and regularly reloading the code from that trusted memory. Notice that some works [DY05, BDK08, DY08] address the problem of soft-errors in self-stabilizing algorithms, but this is out of the scope of this book.

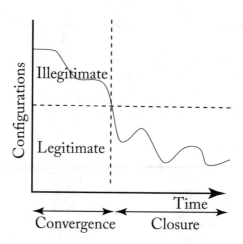

Figure 1.3: Absence of fault in the model.

1.2.2   A LIGHTWEIGHT APPROACH FOR FAULT TOLERANCE

The overhead of self-stabilizing algorithms as compared to non-fault-tolerant algorithms is observable regarding execution time, memory requirement, and exchanged information. It is worth noticing that for many problems, the overhead of the state-of-the-art self-stabilizing algorithms is asymptotically negligible. Actually, self-stabilization is often considered as a *lightweight* fault tolerance technique as compared with the classical robust approach [Tix06]. This is probably due to the fact that self-stabilization follows an *optimistic* approach, while robust algorithms follow a *pessimistic* one [Tel01]. The goal of the *pessimistic* approach is to prevent the system from deviating from its specification, in particular in presence of faulty behaviors, by preceding each step with sufficient checks in order to validate it. By contrast, the *optimistic* approach consists in never suspecting the occurrence of non-expected events such as faults, and thus may cause inconsistent behaviors to happen, but guarantees that any deviation from the specification is temporary.

1.2.3   OTHER ADVANTAGES

Performing a proper and consistent initialization is a complex and critical synchronization task in distributed systems. For example, a large-scale network (e.g., Internet) involves numerous processes that may be geographically far from each other and this makes consistency of initialization particularly hard to obtain. So, self-stabilizing algorithms are very desirable for such systems because self-stabilization requires no kind of initialization.

Furthermore, self-stabilization turns out to be a promising approach for *evolving* networks [BFJ03], i.e., networks in which no communication channel linking the entities is (*a priori*) fixed. Indeed, even if self-stabilizing algorithms are most often designed for static topologies, those dedicated to arbitrary network topologies tolerate, up to a certain extent, some topological changes (i.e., the addition or the removal of communication links or nodes). Precisely, if topological changes are eventually detected locally at involved processes and if the frequency of such events is low enough, then they can be considered as transient faults.

These two latter advantages make self-stabilization naturally suited for *autonomic computing*. The concept of autonomic computing was first used by IBM in 2001 to describe computing systems that are said to be *self-managing* [HM08, KC03]. The spirit of autonomic computing is to capture an extensive collection of concepts related to *self-* capabilities*, e.g., self-organization, self-healing, self-configuration, self-management, self-optimization, self-adaptiveness, or self-repair. Roughly speaking, autonomic computing gathers all techniques allowing a distributed system to adapt to unpredictable changes while hiding intrinsic complexity to operators and users. Therefore, self-stabilization can be seen as a theoretically founded alternative for the design of autonomic systems.

Finally, the fact that self-stabilizing algorithms never deadlock despite the arbitrary configuration of the system makes them easy to compose [Her92b, Tel01]. Consider, for example, two self-stabilizing algorithms A and B such that B takes the output of A as input. A and B can be executed in parallel since eventually A will provide a correct input to B and from that point, the actual convergence of B will be guaranteed.[1]

All these aforementioned advantages make self-stabilization desirable for practical systems. Actually, there already exist self-stabilizing applications deployed in real networks [DOTF94]. Moreover, classical routing protocols have been made self-stabilizing, e.g., a self-stabilizing version of BGP (Border Gateway Protocol), the standard inter-domain routing protocol in the Internet, has been proposed by Chen et al. [CDT05].

1.2.4   RELATIVE DRAWBACKS AND ALTERNATIVES

As mentioned earlier, self-stabilization is a non-masking fault tolerance approach. That is, after transient faults cease there is a finite period of time, called the *stabilization phase*, during which the safety properties of the system are violated. Loss of safety is clearly the main drawback of self-stabilization approach. This is why reducing the *stabilization time*, i.e., the maximum duration of the stabilization phase, definitely remains the primary target of algorithm designers. Another important line of research has been to propose stronger forms of self-stabilization to mitigate the effects of the loss of safety during the stabilization phase. In other words, all these variants of self-stabilization offer extra safety guarantees. For instance, the *fault-containment* [GGHP07] approach additionally ensures that when few (transient) faults hit the system, the faults are both spatially and temporally contained. *Time-adaptive* self-stabilization [KPS99] guarantees a stabilization time linear in the number of faults f, if f does not exceed a given threshold. *Snap-stabilizing* algorithms [CDD$^+$16] recover a correct behavior immediately after transient faults cease.

---

[1]This composition technique, introduced by Herman in [Her92b], is called the *collateral composition*.

Self-stabilizing algorithms are specifically designed to handle transient failures. Consequently, they are not inherently suited for other failure patterns, a.k.a., intermittent failures—i.e., temporary failures having a higher frequency of occurrence than that of transient faults—and permanent failures. Actually, most existing self-stabilizing solutions become totally ineffective in case of permanent failures such as process crashes, or Byzantine failures. However, notice that several self-stabilizing algorithms also support intermittent failures, such as frequent lost, duplication, or reordering of messages, e.g., [DT02, DDT06, DDLV17]. Moreover, strong forms of self-stabilization have been introduced to cope with process crashes, e.g., *fault-tolerant self-stabilization* [BK97, DDF10], and Byzantine faults, e.g., *strict stabilization* [NA02, DMT15].

In self-stabilizing systems, processes cannot locally decide whether the system has globally converged, except for few trivial specifications. Indeed, assume a situation where a process p truly decides, using available local information, that the system is in a legitimate configuration. Then, it is almost always possible to build an illegitimate configuration in which p has access to exactly the same local information. Consequently, p cannot distinguish between the two situations. In the second one, p will take a wrong decision. As a consequence, usually all processes should run their local algorithm forever in order to permanently check whether or not they should update their local state after learning fresh information, e.g., message passing methods for self-stabilization often require the use of heartbeat messages (i.e., control messages that are periodically sent) [APSV91, DDT06]; algorithms implementing such a heartbeat method are said to be *proactive* in the literature. However, notice that Arora and Nesterenko [AN05] mitigated this problem, since they proposed non-proactive, a.k.a. reactive, self-stabilizing solutions for non-trivial problems, such as *mutual exclusion*, where message exchanges eventually stop in absence of further input modification (e.g., in absence of any further request). Yet, their method cannot be generalized since they also show that many problems, like *leader election*, only admit self-stabilizing proactive solutions.

Finally, additional assumptions may be necessary to obtain self-stabilization. For example, a non self-stabilizing data-link protocol can be implemented using only two sequence values [Lyn68]. This latter algorithm, known as the *Alternating Bit Protocol*, works using bounded (actually small) local process memories in message passing where links are assumed to be bidirectional, fair lossy, yet of unbounded capacity. Now, Gouda and Multari [GM91] show that it is impossible to implement a (deterministic) self-stabilizing data-link protocol under such assumptions. However, they also show that the problem becomes self-stabilizingly solvable still with unbounded capacity links, yet assuming infinite process memories. In [Var00], Varghese circumvents the impossibility by proposing a self-stabilizing (deterministic) algorithm, using bounded local process memories, for the case where a bound on link capacity is known by all processes.

1.2.5 EXPRESSIVENESS

The expressiveness of self-stabilization, i.e., characterizing which problems admit a self-stabilizing solution, has been addressed by Katz and Perry [KP93]. They consider message passing systems where links are reliable and have unbounded capacity, and processes are both identified and equipped of infinite local memories. In this model, they propose a characterization of problem specifications admitting a self-stabilizing solution. Namely, they show that a non-stabilizing algorithm can be transformed into a self-stabilizing algorithm for the same specification if and only if its specification is *suffix-closed*. Roughly speaking, a specification is suffix-closed if it excludes any infinite execution which is decomposable into a finite prefix p and a suffix s where a particular non-empty behavior occurs in p, but never in s.

A trivial non suffix-closed specification is the problem of "printing" the infinite sequence 1, 0, 0, 0 ... Such a problem trivially admits no self-stabilizing solution. Indeed, assume an algorithm A that realizes this specification in an execution e (n.b., any self-stabilizing algorithm realizes its specification in at least one execution). By definition, e has an infinite suffix s in which no 1 is ever printed. Then, s is a possible execution, which starts from an arbitrary configuration, and s has no suffix satisfying the specification: consequently A is not self-stabilizing.

It is worth noticing that, even if Katz and Perry consider a message passing model, the impossibility side of their characterization, i.e., the fact that non suffix-closed specifications have no self-stabilizing solution, is independent from the computational model. Indeed, essentially the impossibility holds because processes cannot be confident with their local state due to the arbitrary initialization of the system. In the example, processes cannot decide to never more output 1 because they have no means to remember it has been done before. As a matter of fact, this impossibility result holds even considering a central system, i.e., a single process: in this case, the process has access to the global state of the system directly, without using any mean of communication.

Apart from problems proven impossible by Katz and Perry, many other impossibility results are due to actual features of the considered systems, namely the computational model and/or its assumptions. For example, like for the non fault-tolerant algorithmic, many impossibilities are due to anonymity. Indeed, many classical problems, such as leader election or token passing, have no self-stabilizing solution in a fully anonymous system (refer to [YK96] and [Her90], respectively). Those impossibility results have justified the introduction of weak versions of self-stabilization, such as weak stabilization [Gou01] and probabilistic self-stabilization [IJ90], where those problems become solvable. For example, weak stabilizing algorithms for leader election and token passing are proposed in [DTY15]. Similarly, probabilistically self-stabilizing algorithms for leader election and token passing can be found in [DIM97b] and [IJ90], respectively. These generalizations of self-stabilization are out of the scope of this book; see [DPV11a] for a detailed survey.

1.2.6   TAXONOMY OF THE SELF-STABILIZING LITERATURE

After the seminal work of Dijkstra [Dij73, Dij74], many self-stabilizing algorithms have been proposed to solve various tasks such as *spanning tree constructions* [BPBRT10], *token circulations* [HC93], *unison* [CFG92], and *propagation of information with feedback* [BDPV99a]. The considered problems can be classified in the following categories:

1. computation of distributed structures (also referred to as *self-organization*), such as spanning trees [BPBRT10] or clustering [DDH+16];

2. routing algorithms [CG01, DT01, CDL+13];

3. wave algorithms such as token passing [HC93, DJPV00] and propagation of information with feedback [BDPV99a];

4. synchronization such as unison [GH90] and phase synchronization [HLH04]; and

5. resource allocation problems such as mutual exclusion [Dij73, Dij74] and dining philosophers [HP92].

Those works consider a large variety of *topologies*: complete graphs [DDF10], rings [MK05, BT18], directed or undirected trees [BDPV99a, CT11, TK15, DDLV17], planar graphs [LC10, GK93], arbitrary connected graphs [DGPV01, ACD+17], etc.

The self-stabilizing solutions can be also discriminated by the *level of synchrony* (sequential—like in [Dij73, Dij74], synchronous—like in [GH90], or fully distributed—like in [BDPV99a]) and of *anonymity* (fully anonymous—like in [GH90], rooted—like in [BDPV99a], or identified—like in [DDH+16]) they assume.

Finally, maybe the most important criteria is the *computational model* in which the algorithm is written. So far, three main models have been extensively studied (from the weakest to the stronger): the (classical) *message passing model* [KP93], the *register model* (also called the locally shared memory model with read/write atomicity) [Dol00], and the *atomic-state model* (also called locally shared memory model with composite atomicity) [Dij73, Dij74]. The two last ones are actually abstractions of the message passing model where message exchanges between neighbors are replaced by a direct access to the state of the neighbors. The register model and the atomic-state model differ by their atomicity assumption. In the atomic-state model, each atomic step consists of at least one process (maybe several) reading its state and that of all its neighbors, and updating its own state. In the register model, atomicity is weaker. Each process holds some communication registers it shares with its neighbors and (maybe) some internal, i.e., non-shared, variables. An atomic step consists of one process making internal computation followed by either a read or write action on a communication register.[2] Precisely, a read action

---

[2]The fact that executions are sequential in the register model is not a restriction, it is rather a way to simplify the modeling. Indeed, under such an atomicity, any concurrent step can be simulated by a finite number of sequential steps.

allows the process to get the value of one register owned by a neighbor, while a write action allows the process to update one of its own registers.

The atomic-state model has been introduced by Dijkstra in its primary work on self-stabilization [Dij73, Dij74]. Since then, it is the most commonly used model in self-stabilization. This is why we will focus on this model in the present book. Asynchronism in this model is captured by the notion of *daemon*, an adversary which decides the interleaving of process executions. The power of a daemon is characterized by its *spreading* (e.g., central, locally central, distributed, synchronous) and its *fairness* (e.g., strongly fair, weakly fair, unfair)—refer to [DT11] for a detailed survey. In this book, as a pedagogic approach, we will start by studying a solution assuming a strong daemon and then incrementally consider algorithms accepting weaker and weaker daemons, until dealing with the most general one, i.e., the distributed unfair daemon.

Finally, notice that considering a high-level model such as the atomic-state model is not a restriction, rather a way to simplify both the design and proof of the solutions. Indeed, many proposals, e.g., [AB93, DIM93, Var00], allow to bring all solutions written in the atomic-state model to weaker models, such as the register model or the message passing model. In the last chapter of this book, we will present an overview of methods that can be used to bring solutions from the atomic-state model to the message passing one, or to directly develop message passing solutions.

1.3 ROADMAP OF THIS BOOK

The remainder of this book is organized in seven chapters. Chapters 1–7 deal with the atomic-state model and Chapter 8 is dedicated to the message passing model.

Chapter 2 is devoted to the formal definition of the main computational model used in this book, i.e., the atomic-state model.

In Chapter 3, we study our first self-stabilizing algorithm. This algorithm solves a static problem called the (vertex) *coloring* problem. The proposed solution works in arbitrary anonymous networks, assuming one of the strongest daemon, the locally central unfair daemon. This algorithm is mainly a toy example to illustrate the concepts defined in the previous chapter.

In Chapter 4, we study our first dynamic problem. It is actually a clock synchronization problem called *synchronous unison*. We investigate a self-stabilizing solution to this problem which is designed for synchronous anonymous systems of arbitrary topology.

In Chapter 5, we focus on the general static problem of building a spanning tree. Spanning tree constructions are central in self-stabilization since they are widely used as basic building blocks of more complex self-stabilizing solutions. In this chapter, we focus on the construction of a Breadth-First Search (BFS) spanning tree in a connected rooted network, assuming the weakest scheduling assumption of the atomic-state model, the distributed unfair daemon.

In Chapter 6, we revisit the first self-stabilizing algorithm proposed by Dijkstra in his seminal papers [Dij73, Dij74]. This algorithm solves the token passing problem in any rooted and oriented ring. In particular, we study the impact of the scheduling assumption on its complexity, by considering two cases: the locally central unfair daemon and the distributed unfair daemon.

In Chapter 7, we study a composition method called *hierarchical collateral composition*. Composition is a fundamental design pattern in self-stabilization, as it allows to split the design of a complex algorithm into more simple building blocks. We give a sufficient condition to show the self-stabilization of a composite algorithm under the distributed weakly fair daemon. We then apply this latter result to a simple case study.

Finally, Chapter 8 concludes this book by presenting simple methods to design self-stabilizing algorithms in message passing systems. We consider two main approaches. One is dedicated to static problems, while the other can be applied to any kind of problems, in particular dynamic ones.

CHAPTER 2

Preliminaries

In this chapter, we introduce and formalize definitions and concepts that will be used all along the book. In particular, we will focus on the computational model and the definition of self-stabilization in this model.

2.1 NETWORK

We define a distributed system as a collection of n interconnected computing entities, called processes or nodes, that execute a distributed algorithm (or protocol) to collectively solve a global task. A process can transmit to and get information from a part of other processes. Information exchanges are assumed here to be bidirectional: a process p can obtain information from process q if and only if q can obtain information from p. Henceforth, the communication network, also called topology, is conveniently modeled by a simple undirected graph $G = (V, E)$, where V is the set of processes and E a set of edges $\{p, q\}$ representing the ability of p and q to directly exchange information together. For every edge $\{p, q\}$, p and q are said to be *neighbors*. Every (undirected) edge $\{p, q\}$ actually consists of two arcs: (p, q) (i.e., the directed link from p to q) and (q, p) (i.e., the directed link from q to p).

2.1.1 LOCAL LABELING

We assume that every process p can distinguish its neighbors using a *local labeling*. All labels of p's neighbors are stored into the set $p.\mathcal{N}$. Such a labeling is called *indirect naming* [SK87]. In the reasoning, when it is clear from the context, we use, by an abuse of notation, p to designate both the process p itself, and its corresponding local label in the set $q.\mathcal{N}$ of any of its neighbors q.

2.1.2 GRAPH NOTIONS

Paths

A *path* of length k, or simply a path, in G is any sequence $P = p_0, ..., p_k$ such that for every $0 \leq i < k$, $\{p_i, p_{i+1}\} \in E$. p_0 and p_k are called the extremities of P. Let $P = p_0, ..., p_k$ be a path of G.

- P is *simple* if no edge appears more than once in P, i.e., $\forall 0 \leq i < j < k$, $\{p_i, p_{i+1}\} \neq \{p_j, p_{j+1}\}$.

- P is *elementary* if no vertex appears more than once in P, i.e., $\forall 0 \leq i < j \leq k$, $p_i \neq p_j$.

- P is a *cycle* if P is simple and $p_0 = p_k$.

- P is an *elementary cycle* if P is a cycle and $p_0, \ldots, p_{k-1}$ is an elementary path.

Let $p, q \in V$ be two processes. We denote by $\|p, q\|$ the (hop-)distance between p and q, namely the length of the shortest path between p and q. We call *diameter* of the graph, noted $\mathcal{D}$, the maximum distance between any two processes:

$$\mathcal{D} = \max\{\|p, q\| : p, q \in V\}.$$

We call *closed neighborhood* of process p the subset of processes at distance at most one from p, i.e., p and its neighbors.

Extra Graph Notions

Let δ_p be the *degree of process* p, i.e., the number of edges incident to p in G. The *(maximum) degree of G* is $\Delta = \max_{p \in V} \delta_p$.

- G is *regular* if all its nodes have the same local degree.

- G is *acyclic* if G contains no cycle.

- G is *connected* if for every two nodes p and q there is a path in G linking p to q.

- $G' = (V', E')$ is a *subgraph* of G if $V' \subseteq V$ and $E' \subseteq E$. The *subgraph of G induced by* $V' \subseteq V$ is the graph $G' = (V', E')$ where $E' = \{\{p, q\} \in E : p \in V' \land q \in V'\}$.

- G is a *tree* if G is both acyclic and connected.

2.2   COMPUTATIONAL MODEL

We consider the atomic-state model of computation introduced by Dijkstra [Dij73, Dij74].

A *distributed algorithm* A is a collection of n *local algorithms*, each one operating on a single process: $A = \{A(p) : p \in V\}$ where each process p is equipped with a local algorithm $A(p)$. The local algorithm of p consists of a finite set of locally shared registers—here called *variables*—and a finite set of *actions*—also called *rules* or *guarded commands*— allowing p to update them. Notice that in A, some local algorithms may be different from each other.

2.2.1   VARIABLES

In this model, communications are carried out by the variables. Some of them, like $p.\mathcal{N}$, may be constant inputs from the system in which case their values are predefined. Each process can read its own variables and that of its neighbors, but can write only to its own (non-constant) variables. The *state* of a process is defined by the values of its local variables. A *configuration* of the system is a vector consisting of the states of each process. The set of configurations of A is denoted by $\mathcal{C}_{\mathtt{A}}$, or simply $\mathcal{C}$ when there is no ambiguity. For every configuration γ in $\mathcal{C}$, we denote by $\gamma(p)$ (*resp.* $\gamma(p).x$) the state of process p (resp. the value of the variable x of process p) in configuration γ.

2.2.2 ACTIONS

Each action of local algorithms is of the following form:

$$\langle label \rangle \ :: \ \langle guard \rangle \ \rightarrow \ \langle statement \rangle.$$

Labels are only used to identify actions in the reasoning. A *guard* is a Boolean predicate involving the variables of the process and that of its neighbors. The *statement* is a sequence of assignments on variables of the process. An action can be executed only if its guard evaluates to *true*; in this case, the action is said to be *enabled*. By extension, a process is said to be enabled if at least one of its actions is enabled. We denote by $Enabled(\gamma)$ the subset of processes that are enabled in configuration γ.

2.2.3 STEPS AND EXECUTIONS

Processes run their local algorithm by atomically executing actions. Assume that the current configuration of the system is γ. If $Enabled(\gamma) = \emptyset$, then γ is said to be *terminal* (no more step of A is possible from γ). Otherwise, a *step of* A *in* G is performed as follows: a non-empty subset S of $Enabled(\gamma)$ is nondeterministically activated (or selected); then every process p in S *atomically* executes one of its action enabled in γ,[1] leading the system to a new configuration γ'. The step (of A in G) from γ to γ' is noted $\gamma \xrightarrow[G]{A} \gamma'$: $\xrightarrow[G]{A}$ is the binary relation over the configurations (of A) defining all possible steps of A in G. Precisely, in $\gamma \xrightarrow[G]{A} \gamma'$, for every *activated* process p, $\gamma'(p)$ is set according to the statement of the action executed by p based on the values it reads in γ, whereas $\gamma'(q) = \gamma(q)$ for every non-activated process q. Notice that the $\xrightarrow[G]{A}$ is fully determined by the distributed algorithm A and the topology G on which A is deployed. In this book, we only consider deterministic algorithms, so statements that do not modify the process state are useless: we exclude trivial actions that do not modify the state of the executing process. Hence, whenever a process p executes an action in a step $\gamma \xrightarrow[G]{A} \gamma'$, we have $\gamma(p) \neq \gamma'(p)$, i.e., the set $Activated(\gamma, \gamma')$ of processes activated in $\gamma \xrightarrow[G]{A} \gamma'$ is $\{p \in Enabled(\gamma) \ : \ \gamma(p) \neq \gamma'(p)\}$.

An *execution* of Algorithm A in the network G is a maximal sequence $e = \gamma_0\gamma_1 \cdots \gamma_i \cdots$ of configurations such that $\gamma_{i-1} \xrightarrow[G]{A} \gamma_i$ (and so $\gamma_{i-1} \neq \gamma_i$) for all $i > 0$. The term "maximal" means

---

[1]In case of several enabled actions at an activated process, the choice of the executed action is nondeterministic. However, such situations are usually avoided: most of algorithms are written as a set of locally mutually exclusive actions. Yet, notice that there exists few algorithms, e.g., [HC92], proven self-stabilizing where actions are not locally mutually exclusive.

that the execution e is either infinite, or ends at a *terminal* configuration. Notice that there is no hypothesis on the initial configuration γ_0 of e: γ_0 is arbitrarily chosen in the set of all possible configurations of A.

2.2.4 DAEMONS

Executions are driven by a nondeterministic adversary which models the asynchronism of the system and is called a *daemon*. The daemon decides which enabled processes are activated in a step, and which of their enabled actions are executed. We define a daemon D as a predicate over executions. An execution e is said to be an *execution under the daemon* D if e satisfies D, i.e., $D(e)$ holds. The set of executions of A in G under D is denoted by $\mathcal{E}_{A,G}^D$, or simply $\mathcal{E}$ when A, G, and D are clear from the context. There exist many daemon specifications in the literature. By definition of the model, a daemon can only activate enabled processes and satisfies the following *progress property*, noted $\mathbb{P}$: for every execution $e = \gamma_0 \gamma_1 \cdots \gamma_i \cdots$, e satisfies the predicate $\mathbb{P}(e)$, where

$$\mathbb{P}(e) \stackrel{\text{def}}{=} \forall i > 0, Activated(\gamma_{i-1}, \gamma_i) \neq \emptyset.$$

Daemons satisfying the progress property are also referred to as *proper*. Notice that there are models in which daemons may not be proper, see for example the model given in [DTY15] in which the (distributed) *randomized daemon* is not proper (n.b., this latter daemon activates enabled processes independently and uniformly at random).

Daemons are usually defined as the *conjunction* of their *spreading* and *fairness* properties.

Spreading

The spreading restricts the choice of the daemon at each step obliviously, i.e., without taking past actions into account. It is a safety property in the sense of Alpern and Schneider, see [AS85].

A daemon is *central (or sequential)*, noted $\mathbb{C}$, if it activates exactly one process per step: for every execution $e = \gamma_0 \gamma_1 \cdots \gamma_i \cdots$, e *is an execution under a central (or sequential) daemon* (for short, e is a central—or sequential—execution) if e satisfies the predicate $\mathbb{C}(e)$, where

$$\mathbb{C}(e) \stackrel{\text{def}}{=} \forall i > 0, |Activated(\gamma_{i-1}, \gamma_i)| = 1.$$

A daemon is *locally central*, noted $\mathbb{LC}$, if it never activates two neighbors in the same step: for every execution $e = \gamma_0 \gamma_1 \cdots \gamma_i \cdots$, e *is an execution under a locally central daemon* (for short, e is a locally central execution) if e satisfies the predicate $\mathbb{LC}(e)$, where

$$\mathbb{LC}(e) \stackrel{\text{def}}{=} \forall i > 0, \forall p, q \in Activated(\gamma_{i-1}, \gamma_i), \{p, q\} \notin E.$$

A daemon is *synchronous*, noted $\mathbb{S}$, if it activates every enabled process at each step: for every execution $e = \gamma_0 \gamma_1 \cdots \gamma_i \cdots$, e *is an execution under the synchronous daemon* (for short, e is a synchronous execution) if e satisfies the predicate $\mathbb{S}(e)$, where

$$\mathbb{S}(e) \stackrel{\text{def}}{=} \forall i > 0, Enabled(\gamma_{i-1}) = Activated(\gamma_{i-1}, \gamma_i).$$

Note that, since we consider deterministic algorithms only, every synchronous execution is fully determined by its initial configuration.

A daemon is *distributed*, noted $\mathbb{D}$, if it activates at least one process (maybe more) at each step, i.e, it is not restricted in terms of spreading (except from being proper): every execution is an execution under the distributed daemon; i.e., $\mathbb{D}(e) \stackrel{\text{def}}{=} true$.

Fairness

Fairness allows to regulate the relative execution rate of processes by taking past actions into account. It is a liveness property in the sense of Alpern and Schneider; see [AS85]. We now define the three most popular fairness assumptions of the literature.

A daemon is *strongly fair*, noted $\mathbb{SF}$, if it activates infinitely often all processes that are enabled infinitely often: for every execution $e = \gamma_0 \gamma_1 \cdots \gamma_i \cdots$, *e is an execution under a strongly fair daemon* (for short, *e is a strongly fair execution*) if e satisfies the predicate $\mathbb{SF}(e)$, where

$$\mathbb{SF}(e) \stackrel{\text{def}}{=} \forall p \in V, (\forall i \geq 0, \exists j \geq i, p \in Enabled(\gamma_j)) \Rightarrow (\forall i \geq 0, \exists j > i,$$
$$p \in Activated(\gamma_{j-1}, \gamma_j)).$$

A daemon is *weakly fair*, noted $\mathbb{WF}$, if it eventually activates every continuously enabled process: for every execution $e = \gamma_0 \gamma_1 \cdots \gamma_i \cdots$, *e is an execution under a weakly fair daemon* (for short, *e is a weakly fair execution*) if e satisfies the predicate $\mathbb{WF}(e)$, where

$$\mathbb{WF}(e) \stackrel{\text{def}}{=} \forall i \geq 0, \forall p \in Enabled(\gamma_i), \exists j > i, p \notin Enabled(\gamma_j) \vee p \in Activated(\gamma_{j-1}, \gamma_j).$$

An *unfair* daemon, noted $\mathbb{UF}$, has no fairness constraint, i.e., $\mathbb{UF}(e) \stackrel{\text{def}}{=} true$: it might never select a process unless it is the only enabled one.

Steps Under a Daemon

As we have seen, the spreading assumption may restrict the set of steps that can be performed. We denote by $\underset{G}{\overset{A,D}{\mapsto}}$ the subrelation of $\underset{G}{\overset{A}{\rightsquigarrow}}$ defining the set of possible steps of A in the network G under the daemon D, i.e., $\underset{G}{\overset{A,D}{\mapsto}}$ is the minimal subrelation of $\underset{G}{\overset{A}{\rightsquigarrow}}$ subject to the following condition: for every execution $e = \gamma_0 \gamma_1 \ldots$, $D(e) \Rightarrow \left(\forall i > 0, \gamma_{i-1} \underset{G}{\overset{A,D}{\mapsto}} \gamma_i \right)$. For example, $\underset{G}{\overset{A,C}{\mapsto}} = \left\{ \gamma \underset{G}{\overset{A}{\rightsquigarrow}} \gamma' : |Activated(\gamma, \gamma')| = 1 \right\}$ is the set of possible steps of the algorithm A in the network G under a central daemon. In the sequel, we simply write $\mapsto$ instead of $\underset{G}{\overset{A,D}{\mapsto}}$ when G, A, and D are clear from the context.

Hierarchy of Daemons

The *distributed unfair daemon* is the most general daemon of the model since the conjunction $\mathbb{D}(e) \wedge \mathbb{UF}(e)$ is a tautology. Hence, solutions stabilizing under such an assumption are highly desirable, because they work under any other daemon assumption.

A daemon is D said to be *stronger* than a daemon D' if for every execution e, we have $D(e) \Rightarrow D'(e)$; in this case, D' is said to be *weaker* than D. We denote by $D \succeq D'$ (resp. $D' \preceq D$) the fact that D is stronger that D' (resp. D' is weaker than D). Notice that if D' is weaker than D, then every algorithm that is self-stabilizing assuming D' is also self-stabilizing assuming D. In contrast, every problem that has no self-stabilizing solution under D has no solution under D' too.

By definition, in our model, $\mathbb{D} \wedge \mathbb{UF} \preceq D$, for every daemon D. Other trivial relationships between classical daemons are given in Figure 2.1. Notice in particular that, following the literature, the synchronous daemon appears in the figure without being coupled with any fairness assumption. This is justified by the fact that $\mathbb{S}$ implies any of the (presented) fairness properties.

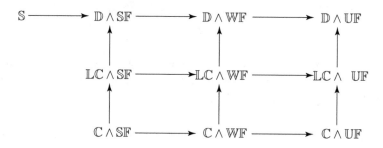

Figure 2.1: Relationships between daemons: $D \succeq D'$ if there is a directed path from D to D'.

2.3   SELF-STABILIZATION

In the original paper of Dijkstra [Dij73, Dij74], self-stabilization is defined rather informally; moreover the definition is not that general (for example, the definition is restricted to sequential systems):

> " *We call the system self-stabilizing if and only if, regardless of the initial state and regardless of the privilege selected each time for the next move, at least one privilege will always be present and the system is guaranteed to find itself in a legitimate state after a finite number of moves.* "

Several, close yet non-equivalent, definitions of self-stabilization exist in the literature. Until now, there is no consensus in the community on a reference definition. However, two main definitions are widely used; see [Dol00, Gho14]. Following a conservative approach (like in [Tel01]), we propose here a strong definition in the sense that every algorithm that is self-stabilizing according to our definition is also self-stabilizing according to the definitions of Dolev [Dol00] and Ghosh [Gho14].

2.3.1   FORMAL DEFINITION

Let A be a distributed algorithm, G be a graph representing some topology, and D be a daemon. Let SP be a specification, i.e., a predicate over executions. We recall that SP is a formal definition of the problem to be solved, in terms of liveness and safety properties.

Definition 2.1   Self-Stabilization.   A is *self-stabilizing for SP in G under D* if there exists a non-empty subset of configurations $\mathcal{L} \subseteq \mathcal{C}$, called the *legitimate* configurations (conversely, $\mathcal{C} \setminus \mathcal{L}$ is called the set of *illegitimate* configurations), such that:

Closure: $\mathcal{L}$ is *closed* (by A in G under D), i.e., $\forall \gamma \in \mathcal{L}$ and $\forall \gamma' \in \mathcal{C}$, if $\gamma \mapsto \gamma'$, then $\gamma' \in \mathcal{L}$.

Convergence: A *converges under D to $\mathcal{L}$ in G*, i.e., $\forall e \in \mathcal{E}, \exists \gamma \in e$ such that $\gamma \in \mathcal{L}$.

Correctness: Under D, SP is *satisfied from* $\mathcal{L}$, i.e., $\forall e \in \mathcal{E}(\mathcal{L})$, $SP(e)$ holds, where $\mathcal{E}(\mathcal{L})$ is the subset of executions of $\mathcal{E}$ that starts from a configuration of $\mathcal{L}$.

Notice that our definition is clearly stronger than the definitions of Dolev [Dol00] and Ghosh [Gho14] since the definition of Dolev is the conjunction of our convergence and correctness properties, while the one of Ghosh is the conjunction of our convergence and closure properties.

2.3.2   SELF-STABILIZATION AND SILENCE

Many self-stabilizing algorithms that construct distributed structures, such as spanning trees, actually achieve an additional property called *silence* [DGS99]. Dolev et al. have introduced this notion in the register model, yet their definition applies independently of any model. A self-stabilizing algorithm is silent if it converges within finite time to a configuration from which the values of the *communication variables* used by the algorithm remain fixed. By communication variable, we mean a buffer variable whose values are transmitted to and/or accessed by a neighbor using the communication primitives (usually send/receive or read/write operations).

Silence is a desirable property. Indeed, as noted in [DGS99], the silent property usually implies more simplicity in the algorithm design. Moreover, a silent algorithm may utilize less communication operations and communication bandwidth.

In our model, an algorithm is *silent* if and only if all its executions in the considered networks and under the considered daemon are finite. Indeed, all variables of a process are actually communication variables since any neighbor can read the whole process state. Considering the atomic-state model, let A be an algorithm that is self-stabilizing for some specification SP (in the network G under the daemon D). Assume that A is also silent. By definition, A has terminal configurations. Let γ be such a terminal configuration. The set of all possible A's executions starting from γ is the singleton $\{\gamma\}$. So, the configuration γ is necessarily legitimate and consequently the execution consisting in just configuration γ satisfies SP. Moreover, every execution of A eventually reaches a terminal configuration. Hence, by

1. choosing the set of legitimate configurations to be the set of the terminal configurations (which is trivially closed), and

2. reformulating a specification SP as a predicate over configurations SP' such that for every configuration γ, $SP'(\gamma)$ holds if and only if γ belongs to the set of executions satisfying SP (n.b., by maximality, if γ is not terminal, then γ is not an execution),

every execution converges to a (legitimate) terminal configuration satisfying SP' if and only if the algorithm is both silent and self-stabilizing for SP, justifying then the following alternative definition of silent self-stabilization in the atomic-state model.

Definition 2.2   Silent Self-Stabilization.   A is *silent and self-stabilizing for the configuration predicate SP' in G under D* if

Termination: $\forall e \in \mathcal{E}$, e is finite.

Partial Correctness: Every terminal configuration satisfies SP'.

2.4   COMPLEXITY

The complexity analysis is the formal study of the performances of an algorithm, in terms of time and space. As for sequential algorithms, an important criteria to compare the order of magnitude of self-stabilizing algorithms' complexity is the types of function that appear in their complexity formulas, e.g., constant, logarithm, or polynomial. However, another important criteria is the dependency w.r.t. the network characteristics, such as its size, its diameter, or its degree. For example, an algorithm A will be (usually) considered as more efficient w.r.t. some complexity measure than an algorithm B if its complexity only depends on local parameter such as its degree, while the complexity of B depends on global parameters such as the network size or the diameter.

2.4.1   TIME COMPLEXITY

Time Units

Three main units of measurement are used in the atomic-state model: the number of *rounds*, *moves*, and *(atomic) steps*.

The complexity in *rounds* evaluates the execution time according to the speed of the slowest processes. This notion has been introduced first by Dolev et al. [DIM93] in the register model, and later adapted by Cournier et al. [CDPV02] for the atomic-state model. It is essentially the transposition to shared memory models of the notion of *time units* (sometime called asynchronous rounds) used in message passing systems [Tel01]. The definition of round uses the concept of *neutralization*: a process v is *neutralized* during a step $\gamma_i \mapsto \gamma_{i+1}$, if v is enabled in γ_i but not in configuration γ_{i+1}, and it is not activated in the step $\gamma_i \mapsto \gamma_{i+1}$. The neutralization of a process v represents the following situation: at least one neighbor of v changes its state between γ_i and γ_{i+1}, and this change effectively makes the guard of all actions of v false. Then, the rounds are inductively defined as follows. The first round of an execution $e = \gamma_0 \gamma_1 \cdots$ is its minimal prefix e' such that every process that is enabled in γ_0 either executes an action or is neutralized during a step of e'. If e' is finite, then the second round of e is the first round of the suffix $\gamma_t \gamma_{t+1} \cdots$ of e starting from the last configuration γ_t of e', and so forth. Notice that, by definition, under a synchronous daemon, at each step exactly one round elapses. Notice also that from any terminal configuration, the next round is trivially defined. However, such trivial rounds are made of no step and so we do not consider them in our studies. Hence, in the following, we say that a prefix of execution *contains X rounds* if it actually consists of X non-trivial rounds, i.e., rounds containing at least one step.

The complexity in *moves* captures the amount of computations an algorithm needs. Indeed, we say that a process *moves* in $\gamma_i \mapsto \gamma_{i+1}$ when it executes an action in $\gamma_i \mapsto \gamma_{i+1}$. So, it is rather a measure of work than a measure of time.

The complexity in *(atomic) steps* essentially captures the same information as the complexity in *moves*. Indeed, the number of moves and the number of steps are closely related: if an execution e contains x steps, then the number y of moves in e satisfies $x \leq y \leq n \cdot x$, where n is the number of processes. Actually, in most of the literature, upper bounds on step complexity are established by proving upper bounds on the number of moves.

The units of measurement presented here do not depend on any system-specific parameter such as the time to perform an elementary instruction in the statement of an action. In that sense, the guidelines are the same as in sequential computing, where time complexity is expressed in terms of number of instructions instead of physical time units. Accordingly, in the atomic-state model, the cost of each round (resp. move/step) is normalized to be one time unit in the analysis, no matter the complexity (in terms of guard evaluation and statement execution) of the actions executed in. So, even if the cost of each action is low in most of the literature (see, for example, the algorithms presented in this book), the designer should always keep this shortcoming in mind to avoid degenerated solutions where, for example, the cost of some actions would be non polynomial. Notice also that, as for distributed non fault-tolerant algorithms in the message passing model, the time complexity analysis of self-stabilizing algorithms in the atomic-state model aims at capturing the cost in communication rather than in internal processing: in distributed systems, internal processing is expected to be negligible as compared to the communication cost.

Stabilization Time

The *stabilization time* is the main time complexity measure to compare self-stabilizing algorithms. The stabilization time of self-stabilizing algorithm is the maximum time (in rounds, moves, or steps) over every execution of $\mathcal{E}$ to reach a legitimate configuration. In the case of silent self-stabilizing algorithms, this measure corresponds to the maximal duration of an execution of $\mathcal{E}$, i.e., the maximal time to reach a terminal configuration.

Time Complexity and Daemons

To obtain practical solutions, the designer usually tries to avoid strong assumptions on the daemon, like for example, assuming all executions are synchronous. Now, when the considered daemon does not enforce any bound on the execution time of processes, then the stabilization time in moves can be bounded only if the algorithm works under an unfair daemon. For example, if the daemon is assumed to be *distributed and weakly fair* (a daemon stronger than the distributed unfair one) and the studied algorithm actually requires the weakly fairness assumption to stabilize, then it is possible to construct executions whose convergence is arbitrarily long in terms of atomic steps (and so in moves), meaning that, in such executions, there are processes whose moves do not make the system progress in the convergence. In other words, these latter processes waste computation power and so energy. Such a situation should be therefore prevented, making the unfair daemon more desirable than the weakly fair one. As a matter of fact, if the daemon is assumed to be weakly fair, then by definition each round is finite. Yet in this case the number of steps in a round can be bounded only if the studied algorithm actually works without this fairness assumption, i.e., under (at least) an unfair daemon with the same spreading assumption.

Problem-Specific Measures

Performances of self-stabilizing algorithms must be also evaluated according to problem-specific measures, e.g., the *waiting time* for resource allocation problems (i.e., the maximum time for a requesting process to enter the critical section), the *cost of a wave* for wave algorithms (see [Cou09] for more complexity metrics about wave algorithms). Usually, these complexities are evaluated starting from a legitimate configuration, following the principle of separation of concerns. Moreover, this allows for the evaluation of the *time overhead* of the self-stabilizing solution, which is evaluated as the ratio between the time complexity of the self-stabilizing algorithm (starting from a legitimate configuration) and the corresponding time complexity of the best known non-self-stabilizing algorithm for the same task.

Notice that for many problems, the time overhead of self-stabilizing algorithms is negligible. For example, most of the self-stabilizing token passing algorithms, e.g., [CDPV06, CDV09a], achieve each full traversal of the network in $O(n)$ rounds, like non-self-stabilizing solution (for which a lower bound in $\Omega(n)$ has been proven), giving then an overhead in $O(1)$.

Time Optimality

Reducing the stabilization time, i.e., the length of the period where safety properties of the specification is violated, is the main objective of self-stabilizing designers. Now, significant time lower bounds have been proven for important classes of specifications, e.g., Genolini et al. considered algorithms that are self-stabilizing for particular non-static specifications and exhibited a lower bound of $\Omega(\mathcal{D})$ rounds on their stabilization time, where $\mathcal{D}$ is the diameter of the network. Time optimal self-stabilizing solutions have been proposed for various problems, e.g., token circulation [PV99], clock synchronization [AKM+93], and spanning tree constructions [KK13]. Notice also that, by definition, the stabilization time is impacted by worst case scenarios. Now, in most cases, transient faults are sparse and their effect may be superficial. Recent research thus focuses on proposing self-stabilizing algorithms that additionally ensure drastically smaller convergence times in favorable cases. In that spirit, several stronger forms of self-stabilization have been proposed, e.g., *fault-containment* [GGHP07], *superstabilization* [DH95], *time-adaptivity* [KPS99], and *safe convergence* [KM06] (see [DPV11b] for a detailed survey).

2.4.2   SPACE COMPLEXITY

The space complexity of algorithms is usually evaluated in terms of *number of (local) states* or *memory requirement*.

Number of States

Let p be a process. The set $LS(p)$ of p's possible (local) states is the Cartesian product of the domain of all its variables. The number of local states $\#LS(p)$ of some process p is the cardinal of $LS(p)$. The number of states (per process) of an algorithm is then $\#LS = \max_{p \in V} \#LS(p)$.

Memory Requirement

The memory requirement $\#MR(p)$ of p is the number of bits it requires to store all its variables, i.e., the sum of the ceiling of the logarithm to the base 2 of the domain size of its variables. The memory requirement (per process) of an algorithm is then equal to $\#MR = \max_{p \in V} \#MR(p)$. Of course, we have the following relationship: $\#MR = \Theta(\log \#LS)$.

Overhead in Space

The overhead in space of a self-stabilizing algorithm consists in studying the ratio between its space complexity and the space complexity of the best known non-self-stabilizing algorithm for the same task. Notice that there are problems, such as Propagation of Information with Feedback in rooted (directed) tree, where self-stabilizing solutions with a space overhead in $O(1)$ have been proposed [BDPV99c].

Space Optimality

Designing efficient self-stabilizing algorithms in terms of space complexity is rather challenging. Several papers investigate space optimality of self-stabilizing algorithms [Her92a, Joh97, BDPV99c]. Notably, there are problems requiring unbounded local process memories, e.g., in the message passing model, a (deterministic) data-link protocol assuming bidirectional fair lossy links with *unbounded capacity* requires infinite process memories [GM91, AB93]. Finally, there are problems where space and time complexities are orthogonal issues: there are self-stabilizing algorithms that are optimal w.r.t. each of them, but not for both. For example, in [BDPV99b], authors show that a self-stabilizing algorithm for propagation of information with feedback in undirected tree cannot be both optimal in space and time, while it can be done separately. Conversely, there exist few algorithms that are optimal both in space and time, e.g., the two snap-stabilizing (depth-first) token circulations respectively designed for oriented and rooted trees proposed in [PV99].

Notice that, in our model, space complexity is of particular interest since variables are locally shared, meaning that variables are continuously read by all neighbors. So, this gives the communication footprint of the algorithm. Besides, the translation of an algorithm from the atomic-state model to the message passing model usually requires the use of heartbeats, where each process regularly transmits (most of) its local state to all its neighbors; see Chapter 8.

CHAPTER 3

Coloring under a Locally Central Unfair Daemon

3.1 THE PROBLEM

In this chapter we address the problem of *(vertex) coloring* in *anonymous* (not necessarily connected) networks. This problem consists for each process in outputing a value, referred to as its *color*, that is different from the colors of all its neighbors.

We consider *anonymous* systems, i.e., systems where all processes have the same program with the same set of possible states. In particular, they have no local parameter (such as an identity) permitting them to be differentiated. In such systems, any two processes cannot be distinguished, unless they have different local degrees. By extension, a distributed algorithm running on an anonymous system is also called an *anonymous (distributed) algorithm*.

Without restricting the power of the daemon, there is no (deterministic) self-stabilizing algorithm able to solve the coloring problem in every anonymous network. Indeed, there are pathological cases, e.g., when the network is a *regular* graph and the execution is synchronous, as shown below. The fact that self-stabilizing coloring is not solvable in some cases where the execution is synchronous forbids the existence of a general solution under the distributed unfair daemon.

Theorem 3.1 *There is no (deterministic) self-stabilizing algorithm for the coloring problem in a regular anonymous graph, assuming a synchronous daemon.*

Proof. (The following proof is illustrated with Figure 3.1.)

Let A be a distributed algorithm. Assume, by the contradiction, that A is self-stabilizing for the coloring problem in some regular anonymous graph (e.g., a ring, like in Figure 3.1) under the synchronous daemon. As all processes are anonymous, they all have the same set of possible local states. Pick any local state a and consider the initial configuration γ_0 where all processes have local state a. Then, in this configuration, the specification of coloring is not satisfied. So, at least one process is enabled. Now, in γ_0, all processes have exactly the same local view of the network (e.g., see Figure 3.1(*i*)), so all processes are enabled. As the daemon is synchronous and the algorithm is deterministic, they all move in the next step $\gamma_0 \mapsto \gamma_1$ to take the same new local state, say b (e.g., see Figure 3.1(*ii*)). So on and so forth, we can make the same reasoning from γ_1. Consequently, there is an infinite synchronous execution of A where in each configuration

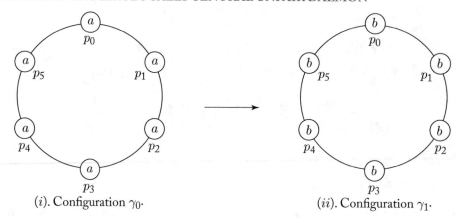

(*i*). Configuration γ_0.   (*ii*). Configuration γ_1.

Figure 3.1: On the impossibility of breaking the symmetry.

all processes have the same local state. This synchronous execution has no suffix satisfying the specification of the coloring, a contradiction.   □

3.2   THE ALGORITHM

Because of the previous impossibility result (Theorem 3.1), we need to make assumptions on the spreading of the daemon; see Figure 2.1 in Section 2.2.4, page 16. This is why we assume here a locally central unfair daemon. (n.b., another way to circumvent this impossibility is to design probabilistic self-stabilizing solutions, e.g., [GT00, BDP+10].)

The algorithm we propose now is essentially the same as the one given by Gradinariu and Tixeuil in [GT00]. It is silent and self-stabilizing. It actually allows to color the network using $K + 1$ colors, where $K \geq \Delta$ (recall that Δ is the maximal degree of the network, as defined in Section 2.1, page 12). Actually, $\Delta + 1$ is the minimum number of colors allowing to solve the problem in any network, no matter the topology is. Indeed any complete graph requires exactly $\Delta + 1$ colors.

The code of the algorithm, called Algorithm Color, is given in Algorithm 3.1. In this algorithm, each process p maintains a single variable $p.c$, called the color (of p), whose domain is $\{0, \ldots, K\}$. Hence, each process p can choose its color among $K + 1 \geq \Delta + 1$ available colors.

The intuitive idea of the algorithm is rather simple. When a process p has at least one neighbor with the same color, the predicate *Conflict*(p) is true: p is enabled to change its color; see Action *Color*. For example, in Figure 3.2(*i*), p and its neighbor q_0 have the same color, 1, and so are both enabled. As the daemon is locally central, if p moves, none of its neighbors does. So, p can simply select a new color among those not used by its neighbors, given by the set *Free*(p) (*Free*(p) is not empty since $K \geq \Delta$). For example, in Figure 3.2(*i*), *Free*(p) = $\{0, 2\}$. Precisely, p sets $p.c$ to the smallest color in *Free*(p). For example, if p moves from the config-

---

Algorithm 3.1 Algorithm `Color`, code for each process p.

Inputs:
  $p.\mathcal{N}$: the set of p's neighbors
  K : an integer such that $K \geq \Delta$

Variable:
  $p.c \in \{0, \dots, K\}$ the color of p

Macros:
  $Used(p)$ $=$ $\{q.c \; : \; q \in p.\mathcal{N}\}$
  $Free(p)$ $=$ $\{0, \dots, K\} \setminus Used(p)$

Predicate:
  $Conflict(p) \stackrel{\text{def}}{=} \exists q \in p.\mathcal{N} \; : \; q.c = p.c$

Action:
  $Color \;\; :: \;\; Conflict(p) \;\; \rightarrow \;\; p.c \leftarrow \min(Free(p))$

---

uration given in Figure 3.2(i), $p.c$ is set to $\min(Free(p)) = 0$, and we have the guarantee that the coloring is locally correct around p, i.e., $Conflict(p)$ no more holds in the next configuration (see Figure 3.2(ii)). Moreover, as no neighbor of p will ever select the color used by p (because for every neighbor q of p, $p.c \in Used(q)$), the property $\neg Conflict(p)$ is then closed along the remainder of execution. Hence, after all initial conflicts are solved, the system is in a terminal configuration where the specification predicate *Colored*, defined below, is satisfied.

Definition 3.2   Let *Colored* $\stackrel{\text{def}}{=} \forall p \in V, \forall q \in p.\mathcal{N}, p.c \neq q.c$.

3.3 PROOF OF SELF-STABILIZATION AND SILENCE

We now show that Algorithm `Color` (see Algorithm 3.1) is silent and self-stabilizing for the configuration predicate *Colored* in any arbitrary (not necessarily connected) anonymous network under the locally central unfair daemon. Recall that silent self-stabilization consists of showing two properties: termination and partial correctness; see Definition 2.2, page 18.

3.3.1 PARTIAL CORRECTNESS

We first show that every terminal configuration is legitimate.

Lemma 3.3   *The predicate Colored holds in every terminal configuration.* (Partial Correctness)

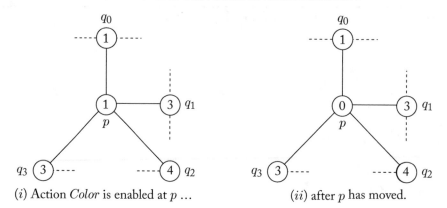

(*i*) Action *Color* is enabled at p ...   (*ii*) after p has moved.

Figure 3.2: Local correction ($K = 4$).

Proof. By definition, in a terminal configuration γ, every process is disabled, so in the case of Algorithm `Color`, the configuration satisfies $\bigwedge_{p \in V} \neg Conflict(p) \equiv Colored$. □

It is worth noticing that the set of configurations satisfying *Colored* exactly coincides with the set of terminal configuration. This property is not required by the definition of silent self-stabilization. Here, it is mainly due to the simplicity of the solution. In most of the cases of the literature, the set of configurations satisfying the specification predicate is a proper superset of the terminal configurations.

3.3.2 TERMINATION

From now on, we consider any execution $e = \gamma_0 \cdots \gamma_i \cdots$ of Algorithm `Color` in an arbitrary graph assuming a locally central unfair daemon.

Below, we first observe that the statement of Action *Color*, the unique action of each process in `Color`, is well defined.

Lemma 3.4   *Let p be a process. In any configuration, for every process p, $Free(p) \neq \emptyset$.*

Proof. By definition, $|Used(p)| \leq \delta_p \leq \Delta \leq K$. Hence, $Free(p) = \{0, \ldots, K\} \setminus Used(p) \neq \emptyset$. □

In the self-stabilizing area, a popular technique to show the termination (or convergence) of an algorithm is to exhibit a *potential function*, also called a *variant function*. A potential function is a function on configurations which is lower bounded and decreases, following a *well-founded* strict ordering,[1] at each step (or round) until reaching that lower bound (e.g., a strictly decreasing non-negative integer function). Consider an expected property P, e.g., the

---

[1]A strict ordering $\succ$ on a set S is *well founded* if there is no infinite descending chain $a_0 \succ a_1 \succ \ldots$ with $a_i \in S$.

configuration is legitimate. The goal is to define a potential function such that while the lower bound is not reached, the configuration of the system satisfies $\neg P$, and once reached, the current configuration is meant to satisfy P. We propose such a function below.

Definition 3.5   Let $Energy(\gamma_i) = |\{p \in V : Conflict(p) \text{ in } \gamma_i\}|$.

The remainder of the proof consists in showing that *Energy* is a potential function. First, by definition of *Conflict*, we have the following observation.

Remark 3.6   Let p be a process and γ_i be a configuration. If $Conflict(p)$ holds in γ_i, then there is at least one neighbor q of p such that $Conflict(q)$ holds in γ_i too.

By definition and Remark 3.6, we can deduce the following remark which, in particular, states that the function *Energy* is both lower and upper bounded.

Remark 3.7   For every configuration γ_i, either $Energy(\gamma_i) = 0$ or $2 \leq Energy(\gamma_i) \leq n$.

Moreover, by definition of the algorithm, we know that once the value of *Energy* is minimum the execution is terminated.

Remark 3.8   For every configuration γ_i, $Energy(\gamma_i) = 0$ if and only if γ_i is terminal.

Below, we show that from step to step, the value of *Energy* cannot increase.

Lemma 3.9   *For every process p and every step $\gamma_i \mapsto \gamma_{i+1}$, if $\neg Conflict(p)$ holds in γ_i, then $\neg Conflict(p)$ holds in γ_{i+1}.*

Proof. First, p is disabled in γ_i, so $\gamma_{i+1}(p).c = \gamma_i(p).c$. Moreover, since $\neg Conflict(p)$ holds in γ_i, for every neighbor q, we have $\gamma_i(q).c \neq \gamma_i(p).c$. Consider now any neighbor q of p. We have two cases.

- *q is not activated in $\gamma_i \mapsto \gamma_{i+1}$.*

    Then, $\gamma_{i+1}(q).c = \gamma_i(q).c \neq \gamma_i(p).c = \gamma_{i+1}(p).c$.

- *q is activated in $\gamma_i \mapsto \gamma_{i+1}$.*

    Then, in γ_i, $p.c \in Used(q)$, and consequently $p.c \notin Free(q)$. Let $x = min(Free(q))$ in γ_i. $x \neq \gamma_i(p).c$. Now, by executing Action *Color*, q sets $q.c$ to x. So, $\gamma_{i+1}(q).c = x \neq \gamma_i(p).c = \gamma_{i+1}(p).c$.

Hence, for every neighbor q, we have $\gamma_{i+1}(q).c \neq \gamma_{i+1}(p).c$, i.e., $\neg Conflict(p)$ still holds in γ_{i+1}. ☐

From Lemma 3.9, we can deduce the following corollary:

Corollary 3.10   *For every two configurations γ_i and γ_j of e such that $i \leq j$, we have $Energy(\gamma_i) \geq Energy(\gamma_j)$.*

We now show that the value of *Energy* decreases at each step.

Lemma 3.11   *For every process p and every step $\gamma_i \mapsto \gamma_{i+1}$, if process p moves in $\gamma_i \mapsto \gamma_{i+1}$, then Conflict($p$) holds in γ_i but not in γ_{i+1}.*

Proof. First, by definition of the algorithm, p is enabled to execute Action *Color* in γ_i, i.e., *Conflict(p)* holds in γ_i.

Then, by definition of the locally central daemon, no neighbor of p is activated in $\gamma_i \mapsto \gamma_{i+1}$, so $\forall q \in p.\mathcal{N}$, $\gamma_{i+1}(q).c = \gamma_i(q).c$.

Moreover, in γ_i, for every neighbor q of p, $q.c$ is in $Used(p)$ and, consequently, $q.c$ is not in $Free(p)$. Let $x = min(Free(p))$ in γ_i. We have $\forall q \in p.\mathcal{N}: x \neq \gamma_i(q).c = \gamma_{i+1}(q).c$. Now, by executing Action *Color*, p sets $p.c$ to x. So, $\forall q \in p.\mathcal{N}$, $\gamma_{i+1}(p).c \neq \gamma_{i+1}(q).c$, i.e., *Conflict($p$)* does not hold in γ_{i+1}.   □

Lemma 3.12   *For every step $\gamma_i \mapsto \gamma_{i+1}$, if $Energy(\gamma_i) = 2$, then exactly one process moves in $\gamma_i \mapsto \gamma_{i+1}$ and $Energy(\gamma_{i+1}) = 0$.*

Proof. In $\gamma_i \mapsto \gamma_{i+1}$, at least one process moves, since the daemon satisfies the progress property. $Energy(\gamma_i) = 2$ means that there are exactly two processes satisfying *Conflict* in γ_i, i.e., exactly two enabled processes in γ_i. Moreover, they are neighbors, by Remark 3.6. Hence, by definition of the locally central daemon, exactly one of them moves in $\gamma_i \mapsto \gamma_{i+1}$. Now, as $Energy(\gamma_i) = 2$, $Energy(\gamma_{i+1}) < 2$, by Lemmas 3.9 and 3.11. Finally, $Energy(\gamma_{i+1}) \neq 1$, by Remark 3.7. So, $Energy(\gamma_{i+1}) = 0$ and we are done.   □

Lemma 3.13   *For every step $\gamma_i \mapsto \gamma_{i+1}$, we have the following.*

1. *$Energy(\gamma_i) \geq 2$, and*

2. *$Energy(\gamma_{i+1}) \leq Energy(\gamma_i) - |Activated(\gamma_i, \gamma_{i+1})|$,   in   particular $Energy(\gamma_{i+1}) < Energy(\gamma_i)$.*

Proof. As at least one process moves at any step (the daemon is proper), at least one process p is enabled in γ_i i.e., it satisfies the predicate *Conflict*, and, by definition, $Energy(\gamma_i) > 0$. Moreover, by Remark 3.7, $Energy(\gamma_i) \geq 2$.

Then, $Energy(\gamma_{i+1}) \leq Energy(\gamma_i) - |Activated(\gamma_i, \gamma_{i+1})|$, by Lemmas 3.9 and 3.11. Again, since the daemon is proper, $|Activated(\gamma_i, \gamma_{i+1})| > 0$, and we have $Energy(\gamma_{i+1}) < Energy(\gamma_i)$. □

Lemma 3.14   *The execution e terminates after at most n − 1 moves.*

Proof. Immediate from Remarks 3.7 and 3.8, and Lemmas 3.12 and 3.13. □

As every step contains at least one move (by the progress property), we have the following.

Corollary 3.15 $\forall e \in \mathcal{E}$, *e is finite.* (Termination)

By Lemma 3.3 and Corollary 3.15, the next Theorem follows.

Theorem 3.16   *Algorithm* Color *is silent and self-stabilizing for configuration predicate Colored (i.e., the coloring specification) in every anonymous network under the locally central unfair daemon.*

3.4   COMPLEXITY ANALYSIS

3.4.1   MEMORY REQUIREMENT

Since every process holds a single variable whose domain is $\{0, \ldots, K\}$ with $K \geq \Delta$, the memory requirement of Algorithm Color is in $\Theta(\log K)$ bits per process. Note also that the bidirectional case, studied here, is very favorable, since the minimum value of K is Δ, while a lower bound in $\Omega(\log n)$ bits per process has been proven for the unidirectional case [BDPT09], even if the daemon is assumed to be (unfair) central.

3.4.2   TIME COMPLEXITY

Stabilization Time in Rounds

Algorithm Color is trivially optimal in round, as shown below.

Theorem 3.17   *The stabilization time of* Color *is at most one round.* (Round Complexity)

Proof. Let $e = \gamma_0 \cdots \gamma_i \cdots$ be any execution of Color in an arbitrary graph assuming a locally central unfair daemon. Let p be a process. If p is disabled in γ_0, then p is disabled forever, by Lemma 3.9. Otherwise, by definition of round, there is a step $\gamma_i \mapsto \gamma_{i+1}$ in the first round where either p moves or p is neutralized. In both cases, p is disabled forever from γ_{i+1}, by Lemmas 3.9 and 3.11. Hence, e lasts at most one round, and we are done. □

Stabilization Time in Moves/Steps

By Lemma 3.14, the stabilization time of Algorithm Color is at most $n - 1$ moves. By definition, this bound also holds for steps. We now show that the bound of $n - 1$ moves/steps is reachable for a wide class of graphs, even if we consider a stronger daemon. From Figure 2.1 (page 16), we know that the central strongly fair daemon is stronger than the locally central unfair daemon. So, a possible behavior of locally central unfair daemon is to mimic this strong daemon. Below, we show that, even in this more favorable case, the bound of $n - 1$ steps is reachable, whenever the network contains an *Hamiltonian path*, i.e., a path that contains each node of the network exactly once.

Theorem 3.18   *In any network containing an Hamiltonian path, there is an execution of* Color, *under the central strongly fair daemon, containing $n - 1$ steps.*

Proof. Let $p_0, \ldots, p_{n-1}$ be an Hamiltonian path of the network. Consider an initial configuration where all processes have the same color. For every $1 \leq i < n$, *Conflict*(p_i) holds until either p_i, or both p_{i-1} and p_{i+1} move. Hence, if the daemon sequentially activates p_0, p_1, ..., p_{n-2}, we know that right after process p_i (with $i \in \{0, \ldots, n - 2\}$) has moved, p_{i+1} is still enabled. Thus, this gives a possible execution that lasts at least $n - 1$ steps, so exactly $n - 1$ steps, by Lemma 3.14. Finally, as this sequential execution terminates, it is trivially strongly fair.   □

In Figure 3.3, we give an example of worst-case execution of Color on a chain network of $n = 6$ processes, i.e., an execution of Color containing exactly five steps. In the initial configuration (i), all processes have color 0 and are enabled. According to the proof of the previous theorem, the daemon first activates node p_0, this latter takes the smallest "available" color, i.e., 1, leading to configuration (ii). Accordingly, p_1, p_2, p_3, and p_4 are then sequentially activated in the next four steps, leading the system to the terminal configuration (vi).

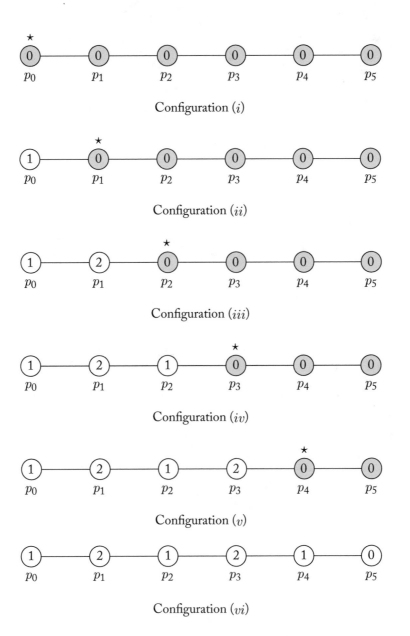

Figure 3.3: Worst-case execution on the chain of $n = 6$ processes: colors are given inside the nodes, enabled processes are filled in gray, nodes activated in the next step are marked with a star.

CHAPTER 4

Synchronous Unison

4.1 THE PROBLEM

In this chapter, we deal with a synchronization problem called *synchronous unison*. Variants of this problem are also known as *asynchronous unison*, *phase* or *barrier synchronization* in the literature. In this problem, each process has a local variable called its *clock*. The liveness property of the problem requires each clock to be incremented infinitely often. The safety property requires every clock has exactly the same value at each instant. Of course, such a strong property can only be implemented in synchronous systems. Hence, to accommodate asynchrony, variants, which mainly differ by their (weaker) safety property, have been proposed. For example, the variant called *asynchronous unison*, and proposed in [CFG92], requires the difference between clocks of every two neighbors to be at most one increment at each instant. Notice that existing solutions also differ by their assumption on the clock definition domain. This domain may be either unbounded like in [GH90], or bounded like in [ADG91]. In the latter case, clocks are periodic and incremented modulo the *period*.

We focus here on a periodic synchronous unison, which requires all clocks to be always equal. We study the solution proposed by Arora et al. [ADG91] and dedicated to connected anonymous synchronous networks. Actually, they consider an even stronger version of the problem in which they additionally impose the clocks to be incremented *at each step*. The period of their unison algorithm is a positive integer, noted m. So, every process p is endowed with a clock variable, noted $p.clock$, whose value is a natural integer in range $[0, m-1]$. An execution e satisfies the synchronous unison specification proposed in [ADG91] if the predicate $SU(e)$ holds, where $SU(e)$ is defined by the conjunction of the following three properties:

- in every configuration of e, all the processes have the same clock value,

- e is infinite, and

- in each step of e, each clock is incremented modulo m.

If $m = 1$, the problem is degenerated since all clocks are always equal to 0. Therefore, we assume $m > 1$ in the sequel.

Notice that the problem we consider here is the strongest clock synchronization paradigm that may be achieved. Trivially, it can be only achieved if the system is synchronous.

4.2 THE ALGORITHM

Algorithm Unison (see Algorithm 4.2 for its formal code) is actually a straightforward adaptation to the atomic-state model defined in this book of the solution proposed in [ADG91]. In Unison, each node p holds a single variable, its clock $p.clock$, and has a single action, noted *Incr*. At each step, p maintains its clock to be the minimum clock value in its closed neighborhood (i.e., the neighborhood of p including p itself) incremented by one modulo m. The constant parameter m (a.k.a., the period) is required to satisfy $m \geq \max\{2, 2D - 1\}$. Once the system has stabilized, $p.clock$ is incremented modulo m at each step thanks to Action *Incr*.

Algorithm 4.2 Algorithm Unison, code for each process p.

Inputs:
  $p.\mathcal{N}$: the set of p's neighbors
  m : an integer such that $m \geq \max\{2, 2D - 1\}$

Variable:
  $p.clock \in \{0, \ldots, m - 1\}$: the clock of p

Macro:
  $NewClockValue(p) \quad = \quad \big(\min \left(\{q.clock : q \in p.\mathcal{N}\} \cup \{p.clock\} \right) + 1 \big) \mod m$

Action:
  $Incr \quad :: \quad p.clock \neq NewClockValue(p) \quad \rightarrow \quad p.clock \leftarrow NewClockValue(p)$

An example of execution of Algorithm Unison is proposed in Figure 4.1. In this example, the network diameter is $D = 3$. Moreover, we set m to $10 \geq \max\{2, 2D - 1\}$. The label, next to each node, gives the successive clock values of the node. The leftmost value is the initial clock value of the node. The next to the right is the clock value after one step, and so on. The rightmost value is the clock value after four steps. For example, the initial clock value of the black node at the bottom of the picture is 7. After one step, its clock value is 1. After one more step, its clock is equal to 2, and so on. In the first step, the black node switches from clock value 7 to clock value 1 because $\{2, 7, 0, 7\}$ is the current multiset of the clock values in its closed neighborhood and

$$1 = \big(\min\{2, 7, 0, 7\} + 1 \big) \mod 10.$$

Notice that, after three synchronous steps, the network is fully synchronized since every node has the clock value 3. Moreover, in the next synchronous step, all clocks are incremented to 4 and so remain fully synchronized, etc.

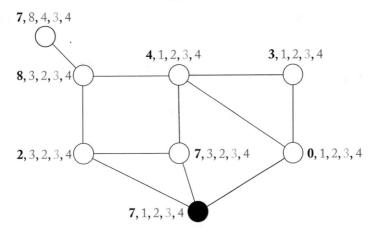

Figure 4.1: Fragment of execution of Algorithm Unison.

4.3   CORRECTNESS AND TIME COMPLEXITY

We now show that Algorithm Unison is self-stabilizing for the specification SU in any connected anonymous network under the synchronous daemon, provided that $m \geq \max\{2, 2D - 1\}$.

4.3.1   CLOSURE AND CORRECTNESS

We define the set *Synced* $\subseteq C$ of legitimate configurations as the subset of configurations where all the clocks have the same value, i.e.,

$$Synced \stackrel{\text{def}}{=} \{\gamma \in C : \forall p, q \in V, \gamma(p).clock = \gamma(q).clock\}.$$

Notice that the set of legitimate configurations defined here is the exact set of configurations where the safety of the problem is satisfied. Such a strong property is not required by the definition of self-stabilization. Actually, in general, to obtain (maybe more easily) the closure property, legitimate configurations of a given algorithm are usually defined as a proper subset of its configurations satisfying the safety of the considered problem. However, the definition of a set of legitimate configuration should be carefully addressed since choosing a too restrictive set of legitimate configurations may lead to an overestimated stabilization time.

Using *Synced* as set of legitimate configurations, the closure and correctness properties of self-stabilization (see Definition 2.1, page 17) trivially hold. Indeed, consider any configuration γ in *Synced*. By definition, every clock has the same value, say $c \in \{0, \ldots, m - 1\}$, in γ. So, in γ, *NewClockValue*(p) is equal to $(c + 1) \mod m$ for every process p. Then, as $(c + 1) \mod m \neq c$ (since $m > 1$), every process is enabled and after a synchronous step, the new configuration is still in *Synced*, since every process has the same clock value $(c + 1) \mod m$. Hence, Lemma 4.1 follows.

Lemma 4.1 *Synced is closed and every execution of* `Unison` *under a synchronous daemon initiated in Synced satisfies SU (i.e., $\forall e \in \mathcal{E}(Synced)$, SU(e) holds).* (Closure and Correctness)

Note that this result is true for any $m > 1$, even if the graph is disconnected.

4.3.2 CONVERGENCE AND COMPLEXITY

We now prove the convergence property of self-stabilization (see Definition 2.1, page 17), i.e., every execution reaches a configuration in *Synced* within a finite number of steps.

Recall that we assume the network $G = (V, E)$ is of arbitrary connected topology. The network diameter is denoted by $\mathcal{D}$. The parameter m is a constant integer satisfying $m \geq \max\{2, 2\mathcal{D} - 1\}$.

First, note that if $\mathcal{D} = 0$, then the network consists of a single node, which is trivially synchronized with itself. Hence, from now on, we assume that $\mathcal{D} > 0$ and consider an arbitrary synchronous execution $e = \gamma_0 \gamma_1 \cdots \gamma_i \cdots$ of Algorithm `Unison`.

Lemma 4.2 *e is infinite.*

Proof. Let γ_i be any configuration of e. Let p be a process such that $\gamma_i(p).clock = \min\{\gamma_i(q).clock : q \in V\}$. By definition, $\min\{\gamma_i(q).clock : q \in p.\mathcal{N}\} \geq \gamma_i(p).clock$. So, $\min(\{\gamma_i(q).clock : q \in p.\mathcal{N}\} \cup \{\gamma_i(p).clock\}) = \gamma_i(p).clock$. Consequently, in γ_i, $NewClockValue(p) = (p.clock + 1) \mod m \neq p.clock$ since $m \geq 2$ and we are done. $\square$

Consider now the prefix $\gamma_0 \cdots \gamma_{\mathcal{D}-1}$ of e, which is well defined by Lemma 4.2. We split the proof of convergence into the following two cases according to the content of $\gamma_0 \cdots \gamma_{\mathcal{D}-1}$:

1. either no configuration in $\gamma_1 \cdots \gamma_{\mathcal{D}-1}$ contains a zero clock value, i.e., $\forall i \in \{1, \ldots, \mathcal{D} - 1\}, \forall p \in V, \gamma_i(p).clock \neq 0$; or

2. at least one configuration contains a zero clock value, i.e., $\exists i \in \{1, \ldots, \mathcal{D} - 1\}, \exists p \in V, \gamma_i(p).clock = 0$.

Case 1

The outline of the proof is as follows. Consider a process p such that $p.clock = \alpha$ is minimum in γ_0. First, remark that p holds the minimum clock value present in Configuration γ_i with $i \in \{0, \ldots, \mathcal{D} - 1\}$ (precisely, $\alpha + i$) since all clocks are strictly positive in $\gamma_1 \cdots \gamma_{\mathcal{D}-1}$ (n.b., some clocks may be equal to zero in γ_0); see Lemma 4.3. Moreover, after one step from γ_0, the clock of each p's neighbor will adopt the minimum clock value $\alpha + 1$ of the current configuration γ_1 (i.e., the new value of $p.clock$); after two steps, every process within distance two from p will also adopt the minimum clock value $\alpha + 2$ of the current configuration γ_2, and so on (cf.

Lemma 4.4). Hence, after $\mathcal{D} - 1$ steps, every process, except maybe some at distance $\mathcal{D}$ of p, holds the same clock value: the minimum clock value $\alpha + \mathcal{D} - 1$ present in configuration $\gamma_{\mathcal{D}-1}$. Consequently, in $\gamma_{\mathcal{D}-1}$, every process has the minimum clock value $\alpha + \mathcal{D} - 1$ present in its closed neighborhood. Hence, the clock of each process is equal to $(\alpha + \mathcal{D}) \bmod m$ in $\gamma_{\mathcal{D}}$, i.e., $\gamma_{\mathcal{D}} \in Synced$, see Lemma 4.5. We now formalize and show this sketch of proof.

Lemma 4.3 *Assume that $\gamma_0 \cdots \gamma_{\mathcal{D}-1}$ satisfies Case 1. Let $p \in V$ be any process with minimum clock value in γ_0. Then, p still holds the minimum clock value during the next $\mathcal{D} - 1$ steps, i.e., for every $k \in \{0, \ldots, \mathcal{D} - 1\}$, we have $\gamma_k(p).clock = \min\{\gamma_k(x).clock \; : \; x \in V\}$.*

Proof. First, if $\mathcal{D} = 1$, then the lemma trivially holds by definition of p and k. Assume now that $\mathcal{D} > 1$. Below, we show the lemma in this case by induction on k.

Base case: The case $k = 0$ is trivial by definition of k.

Induction Hypothesis: Assume that the property holds for some $k \in \{0, \ldots, \mathcal{D} - 2\}$, i.e., for every $i \in \{0, \ldots, k\}$, $\gamma_i(p).clock = \min\{\gamma_i(x).clock \; : \; x \in V\}$.

Induction Step: We now show the property for $k + 1$. Let $\alpha = \gamma_k(p).clock$. By induction hypothesis, $\alpha = \min\{\gamma_k(x).clock \; : \; x \in V\}$. So, since $\gamma_0 \cdots \gamma_{\mathcal{D}-1}$ satisfies Case 1, we have $NewClockValue(p) = \alpha + 1$ (in particular, $Incr$ is enabled at p in γ_k) and $NewClockValue(q) \geq \alpha + 1$, for every process $q \neq p$. Hence, since the execution is synchronous, we have $\gamma_{k+1}(p).clock = \alpha + 1 \leq \gamma_{k+1}(q).clock$ for every process $q \neq p$ (regardless of whether or not $Incr$ is enabled at q in γ_k), and we are done.

$\square$

Lemma 4.4 *Assume that $\gamma_0 \cdots \gamma_{\mathcal{D}-1}$ satisfies Case 1. Let $p \in V$ be any process with minimum clock value in γ_0. For every $k \in \{0, \ldots, \mathcal{D} - 1\}$, for every process q such that $\|p, q\| \leq k$, we have:*

$$\gamma_k(q).clock = \min\{\gamma_k(x).clock \; : \; x \in V\}.$$

Proof. If $\mathcal{D} = 1$, we have $k = 0$ and for every process q such that $\|p, q\| \leq k$, $p = q$, hence the result trivially holds by definition of p.

We now assume $\mathcal{D} > 1$ and we prove the lemma by induction on k.

Base case: For $k = 0$, again, the result trivially holds.

Induction Hypothesis: Assume that the property holds for some $k \in \{0, \ldots, \mathcal{D} - 2\}$, i.e., for every process q such that $\|p, q\| \leq k$, $\gamma_k(q).clock = \min\{\gamma_k(x).clock \; : \; x \in V\}$.

Induction Step: We now show the property for $k + 1$. Let $\alpha = \min\{\gamma_k(x).clock : x \in V\}$. By induction hypothesis, for every process q such that $\|p, q\| \leq k + 1$, either $\|p, q\| \leq k$ and $\gamma_k(q).clock = \alpha$, or $\exists x \in q.\mathcal{N}$ such that $\|p, x\| = k$ and so, $\gamma_k(x).clock = \alpha$. Thus, since $\gamma_0 \cdots \gamma_{D-1}$ satisfies Case 1, $NewClockValue(q) = \alpha + 1$ in γ_k for every process q such that $\|p, q\| \leq k + 1$. As e is a synchronous execution, for every process q such that $\|p, q\| \leq k + 1$, we have $\gamma_{k+1}(q).clock = \alpha + 1$. In particular, $\gamma_{k+1}(p).clock = \alpha + 1$ since $\|p, p\| = 0 \leq k + 1$. Now, by Lemma 4.3, $\gamma_{k+1}(p).clock = \alpha + 1 = \min\{\gamma_{k+1}(x).clock : x \in V\}$. Hence, for every process q such that $\|p, q\| \leq k + 1$, we have $\gamma_{k+1}(q).clock = \alpha + 1 = \min\{\gamma_{k+1}(x).clock : x \in V\}$, and we are done.

$\square$

Lemma 4.5   *If* $\gamma_0 \cdots \gamma_{D-1}$ *satisfies Case 1, then* $\gamma_D \in$ *Synced.*

Proof. Let α be the minimum clock value in γ_{D-1}, i.e., $\alpha = \min\{\gamma_{D-1}(x).clock : x \in V\}$. By Lemma 4.4 and by definition of D, every process p satisfies $p.clock = \alpha \vee \exists q \in p.\mathcal{N}, q.clock = \alpha$ in γ_{D-1}. So, $NewClockValue(q) = (\alpha + 1) \bmod m$ in γ_{D-1}. Hence, as the execution is synchronous, for every process p, $p.clock = (\alpha + 1) \bmod m$ in γ_D, i.e., $\gamma_D \in$ *Synced*. $\square$

Case 2

The outline of the proof is as follows. In this case, there is at least one configuration γ_i, with $i \in \{1, \ldots, D - 1\}$, and a process p such that $\gamma_i(p).clock = 0$. After one step from γ_i, the clocks of all processes in the closed neighborhood of p have values 0 or 1. After two steps from γ_i, the clocks of all processes at distance at most 2 from p have values 0, 1, or 2, and so forth (cf. Lemma 4.6). After at most $D - 1$ steps from γ_i, the value of the clock of each process at distance at most $D - 1$ from p belongs to $\{0, \ldots, D - 1\}$. In other words, every process has a clock value in its closed neighborhood that belongs to $\{0, \ldots, D - 1\}$. Consequently, the clock value of every process will belong to $\{1, \ldots, D\}$ after one more step; see Lemma 4.7. Let $j \leq i + D - 1$ such that $\gamma_{j+1}(q).clock \in \{1, \ldots, D\}$ for every process q, i.e., after one more step. Then, $\gamma_j \cdots \gamma_{j+D-1}$ necessarily satisfies Case 1, see Lemma 4.8. Hence, we retrieve Case 1, and we can conclude that convergence occurs at the latest in configuration γ_{j+D} in Case 2. Since $i \leq D - 1$ and $j \leq i + D - 1$, this gives a stabilization time in at most $3D - 2$ steps (resp. rounds) for Case 2; see Lemma 4.9. We now formalize and show this sketch of proof.

Lemma 4.6   *Assume that* $\gamma_0 \cdots \gamma_{D-1}$ *satisfies Case 2. Let* γ_i, *with* $i \in \{1, \ldots, D - 1\}$, *be a configuration and* p *be a process such that* $\gamma_i(p).clock = 0$. *For every* $k \in \{0, \ldots, D\}$, *for every process* q *such that* $\|p, q\| \leq k$, *we have:*

$$\gamma_{i+k}(q).clock \leq k.$$

Proof. We prove this lemma by induction on k. The proof essentially follows the same lines as the proof of Lemma 4.5.

Base case: Case $k = 0$ is trivial since $\gamma_i(p).clock = 0$ by hypothesis.

Induction Hypothesis: Assume that the property holds for some $k \in \{0, \ldots, \mathcal{D} - 1\}$, i.e., for every process q such that $\|p, q\| \leq k$, $\gamma_{i+k}(q).clock \leq k$.

Induction Step: We now show the property for $k + 1$.

By induction hypothesis, for every process q such that $\|p, q\| \leq k + 1$, either $\|p, q\| \leq k$ and $\gamma_{i+k}(q).clock \leq k$, or $\exists x \in q.\mathcal{N}$ such that $\|p, x\| = k$ and so, $\gamma_{i+k}(x).clock \leq k$. So, $NewClockValue(q) \leq k + 1$ in γ_{i+k}, for every process q such that $\|p, q\| \leq k + 1$. Hence, since the execution is synchronous, $\gamma_{i+k+1}(q).clock \leq k + 1$, for every process q such that $\|p, q\| \leq k + 1$, and we are done.

$\square$

Lemma 4.7 *Let γ_i be any configuration of e. If there exists a process p such that $\forall q \in V, \|p, q\| \leq \mathcal{D} - 1 \Rightarrow \gamma_i(q).clock \in \{0, \ldots, \mathcal{D} - 1\}$, then $\forall q \in V, \gamma_{i+1}(q).clock \in \{1, \ldots, \mathcal{D}\}$.*

Proof. Let q be any process. By definition, either $\|q, p\| < \mathcal{D}$, or $\|q, p\| = \mathcal{D}$ and $\exists x \in q.\mathcal{N}$ such that $\|x, p\| = \mathcal{D} - 1$. So, there is a process x in the closed neighborhood of q such that $\gamma_i(x).clock \in \{0, \ldots, \mathcal{D} - 1\}$. Let α be the value of $\min(\{x.clock : x \in q.\mathcal{N}\} \cup \{q.clock\}) + 1$ in γ_i. We have then $\alpha \in \{1, \ldots, \mathcal{D}\}$. Now, since $\mathcal{D} > 0$, $\alpha < \max\{2, 2\mathcal{D} - 1\} \leq m$. Hence, $NewClockValue(q) = \alpha \in \{1, \ldots, \mathcal{D}\}$ in γ_i and, consequently, since the execution is synchronous, $\gamma_{i+1}(q).clock \in \{1, \ldots, \mathcal{D}\}$, and we are done. $\square$

Lemma 4.8 *Let γ_i be any configuration of e. If $\forall p \in V, \gamma_i(p).clock \in \{1, \ldots, \mathcal{D}\}$, then $\forall k \in \{0, \ldots, \mathcal{D} - 2\}, \forall p \in V, \gamma_{i+k}(p).clock(\in \{1 + k, \ldots, \mathcal{D} + k\}) > 0$.*

Proof. We show this lemma by induction on k. The proof essentially follows the same lines as the proof of Lemma 4.7.

Base case: Case $k = 0$ is trivial.

Induction Hypothesis: Assume that the property holds for some $k \in \{0, \ldots, \mathcal{D} - 3\}$, i.e., if $\forall p \in V, \gamma_i(p).clock \in \{1, \ldots, \mathcal{D}\}$, then $\forall p \in V, \gamma_{i+k}(p).clock(\in \{1 + k, \ldots, \mathcal{D} + k\}) > 0$.

Induction Step: Assume that $\forall p \in V, \gamma_i(p).clock \in \{1, \ldots, \mathcal{D}\}$ and consider the case $k + 1$.

Let q be any process. Let α the value of $\min(\{x.clock : x \in q.\mathcal{N}\} \cup \{q.clock\}) + 1$ in γ_{i+k}. By induction hypothesis, $\forall p \in V, \gamma_{i+k}(p).clock \in \{1 + k, \ldots, \mathcal{D} + k\}$. So, $\alpha \in \{k + 2, \ldots, \mathcal{D} + k + 1\}$. Now, since $k \leq \mathcal{D} - 3$, $\mathcal{D} + k + 1 \leq 2\mathcal{D} - 2 < \max\{2, 2\mathcal{D} - 1\} \leq m$. Hence, $NewClockValue(q) = \alpha(\in \{k + 2, \ldots, \mathcal{D} + k + 1\}) > 0$ in γ_{i+k} and, consequently, after since the execution is synchronous, $\gamma_{i+k+1}(q).clock \in (\{k + 2, \ldots, \mathcal{D} + k + 1\}) > 0$, and we are done.

$\square$

Lemma 4.9   *If $\gamma_0 \cdots \gamma_{\mathcal{D}-1}$ satisfies Case 2, then $\gamma_{3\mathcal{D}-2} \in Synced$.*

Proof.

1. Since $\gamma_0 \cdots \gamma_{\mathcal{D}-1}$ satisfies Case 2, there exist $i \in \{1, \ldots, \mathcal{D} - 1\}$ and a process p such that $\gamma_i(p).clock = 0$.

2. $\forall q \in V$ such that $\|q, p\| \leq \mathcal{D} - 1$, $\gamma_{i+\mathcal{D}-1}(q).clock \leq \mathcal{D} - 1$, by applying Lemma 4.6 with $k = \mathcal{D} - 1$.

3. By 2 and Lemma 4.7, $\forall q \in V$, $\gamma_{i+\mathcal{D}}(q).clock \in \{1, \ldots, \mathcal{D}\}$.

4. By 3 and Lemma 4.8, $\forall q \in V$, $\forall k \in \{0, \ldots, \mathcal{D} - 2\}$, $\gamma_{i+\mathcal{D}+k}(q).clock > 0$.

   Hence, $\gamma_{i+\mathcal{D}-1} \cdots \gamma_{i+2\mathcal{D}-2}$ satisfies Case 1.

5. Thus, $\gamma_{i+2\mathcal{D}-1} \in Synced$ by 4 and Lemma 4.5.

   Now, since $i \leq \mathcal{D} - 1$ and $Synced$ is closed (Lemma 4.1), $\gamma_{3\mathcal{D}-2} \in Synced$, and we are done.

$\square$

Overall Convergence and Self-Stabilization

Lemma 4.10   *The execution e reaches Synced in at most $3\mathcal{D} - 2$ steps.* (Convergence).

Proof. If $\gamma_0 \cdots \gamma_{\mathcal{D}-1}$ satisfies Case 1, then e reaches $Synced$ in at most $\mathcal{D} \leq 3\mathcal{D} - 2$ steps, since $\mathcal{D} > 0$ (see Lemma 4.5). Otherwise, e reaches $Synced$ in at most $3\mathcal{D} - 2$ steps, by Lemma 4.9.

$\square$

By Lemmas 4.10 and 4.1, Theorem 4.11 follows.

Theorem 4.11   *If $m \geq \max\{2, 2D - 1\}$, then Algorithm* Unison *is self-stabilizing for SU in a connected graph under the synchronous daemon. Its stabilization time is at most $3D - 2$ steps (resp. rounds).*

Notice that if we apply the proof given in the original paper [ADG91] to show the self-stabilization of Algorithm Unison in our model, then m is required to strictly greater than $2D$ and we obtain a bound of at most $3D$ steps for the stabilization time. Hence, our proof allows to obtain tighter bounds for both m and the stabilization time.

A Worst-Case Execution

The mechanism of Unison is based on the propagation of clock values along shortest paths. So, we focus below on line graphs, but our worst-case scheme can be generalized to many other topologies. We illustrate our construction with a line of 6 nodes (so of diameter $D = 5$; see Figure 4.2).

We consider any line graph $p_0, \ldots, p_D$ with diameter $D > 1$, i.e., any graph $L = (V, E)$ where $V = \{p_0, \ldots, p_D\}$ and $E = \{\{p_i, p_{i+1}\} : i \in \{0, \ldots, D - 1\}\}$. Let m be any integer such that $m \geq 2D - 1$ (n.b., since $D > 1$, $m > 2$). We consider the initial configuration γ_0 defined as follows:

- $p_0.clock = m - 2D + 2$ and $\forall i \{1, \ldots, D\}$, $p_i.clock = m - D + 1$.

See, for example, the initial configuration in Figure 4.2.

Figure 4.2: Initial configuration γ_0 in a line graph of 6 nodes with $m = 2D - 1 = 9$.

From this initial configuration γ_0, the next $D - 1$ steps give the following configurations. (See Configurations γ_1 to γ_4 in Table 4.1.)

- In every configuration γ_i with $i \in \{1, \ldots, D - 1\}$, for every process p_j with $j \in \{0, \ldots, i\}$, $p_j.clock = m - 2D + 2 + i$, and for every process p_k with $k \in \{i + 1, \ldots, D\}$, $p_k.clock = (m - D + i + 1) \bmod m$.

In particular, in γ_{D-1}, $p_0.clock = m - D + 1 \geq D > 0$ and $p_D.clock = 0$. So, $\gamma_{D-1} \notin$ *Synced*, i.e., the system has not yet converged.

Next $D - 1$ steps give the following configurations. (See Configurations γ_5 to γ_8 in Table 4.1.)

- In every configuration γ_i with $i \in \{D, \ldots, 2D - 2\}$, for every process p_j with $j \in \{0, \ldots, 2D - 2 - i\}$, $p_j.clock = (m - 2D + i + 2) \bmod m$, and for every process p_k with $k \in \{2D - 1 - i, \ldots, D\}$, $p_k.clock = i - D + 1$.

In particular, in γ_{2D-2}, $p_0.clock = 0$ and $p_D.clock = D - 1 > 0$. So, $\gamma_{2D-2} \notin Synced$, i.e., the system has not yet converged.

Next D steps give the following configurations. (See Configurations γ_9 to γ_{13} in Table 4.1.)

- In every configuration γ_i with $i \in \{2D - 1, \ldots, 3D - 3\}$, for every process p_j with $j \in \{0, \ldots, i - 2D + 2\}$, $p_j.clock = i - 2D + 2$, and for every process p_k with $k \in \{i - 2D + 3, \ldots, D\}$, $p_k.clock = i - D + 1$.

  In particular, in γ_{3D-3}, for every process p_j with $j \in \{0, \ldots, D - 1\}$, $p_j.clock = D - 1$ and $p_D.clock = 2D - 2 > D - 1$ since $D > 1$. So, $\gamma_{3D-3} \notin Synced$, i.e., the system has not yet converged.

- However, since $\gamma_{3D-3}(p_D).clock > \gamma_{3D-3}(p_{D-1}).clock$, we have the guarantee that the configuration will be legitimate in γ_{3D-2}. Indeed, in γ_{3D-2}, for every process p_j with $j \in \{0, \ldots, D\}$, $p_j.clock = D$.

Table 4.1: An execution that converges in $3D - 2 = 13$ steps with $D = 5$ and $m = 2D - 1 = 9$

	p_0	p_1	p_2	p_3	p_4	p_5
γ_0	1	5	5	5	5	5
γ_1	2	2	6	6	6	6
γ_2	3	3	3	7	7	7
γ_3	4	4	4	4	8	8
γ_4	5	5	5	5	5	0
γ_5	6	6	6	6	1	1
γ_6	7	7	7	2	2	2
γ_7	8	8	3	3	3	3
γ_8	0	4	4	4	4	4
γ_9	1	1	5	5	5	5
γ_{10}	2	2	2	6	6	6
γ_{11}	3	3	3	3	7	7
γ_{12}	4	4	4	4	4	8
γ_{13}	5	5	5	5	5	5

Hence, $\gamma_{3D-2} \in Synced$, i.e., the execution stabilizes in exactly $3D - 2$ steps. This result implies that the upper bound on the stabilization time given in Theorem 4.11 is tight since it is reachable in line networks, whatever the choice of the value for the parameter m (of course, provided that $m \geq \max\{2, 2\mathcal{D} - 1\}$).

Theorem 4.12   *For every diameter $\mathcal{D} > 1$, for every $m \geq \max\{2, 2\mathcal{D} - 1\}$, there exists a synchronous execution of* Unison *on a line of $\mathcal{D} + 1$ processes that converges in $3\mathcal{D} - 2$ steps.*

4.3.3 MEMORY REQUIREMENT

Every process holds a single variable *clock* which is a natural integer in range $\{0, \ldots, m - 1\}$ with $m \geq \max\{2, 2\mathcal{D} - 1\}$, i.e., m is in $\Omega(\mathcal{D})$. Hence, the memory requirement of the algorithm is in $\Theta(\log m)$ bits per process.

We now investigate the tightness of m. Our answer is partial. Indeed, we show below that there exist non converging executions for any even value of m in $\{2, \ldots, 2\mathcal{D} - 2\}$, so in particular for the very first value smaller than $\max\{2, 2\mathcal{D} - 1\}$.

Again we consider a line network of diameter $\mathcal{D} > 1$. Let X be any value in $\{1, \ldots, \mathcal{D} - 1\}$. We now exhibit a non converging synchronous execution of Unison for $m = 2(\mathcal{D} - X)$, i.e., any even value in $\{2, \ldots, 2\mathcal{D} - 2\}$.

The initial configuration γ_0 is defined as follows:

- $\forall i \{0, \ldots, X - 1\}$, $p_i.clock = 0$ and $\forall j \{X, \ldots, \mathcal{D}\}$, $p_j.clock = \frac{m}{2}$.

See for example, the initial configuration in Figure 4.3.

Figure 4.3: Initial configuration γ_0 in a line graph of 5 nodes with $X = 1$ and so $m = 2(\mathcal{D} - X) = 8$.

Then, the execution loops back to the initial configuration every m steps (recall that m is even).

- In every configuration γ_i with $i \in \{1, \ldots, \frac{m}{2}\}$, $\forall j \in \{0, \ldots, i + X - 1\}$, $p_i.clock = i$ and $\forall k \in \{i + X, \ldots, \mathcal{D}\}$, $p_j.clock = \left(\frac{m}{2} + i\right) \bmod m$.

  In particular, in $\gamma_{\frac{m}{2}}$, for every process p_j with $j \in \{0, \ldots, \mathcal{D} - 1\}$, $p_j.clock = \frac{m}{2} > 0$, and $p_\mathcal{D}.clock = 0$ and. So, $\gamma_{\frac{m}{2}} \notin Synced$.

  (See Configurations γ_1 to γ_4 in Figure 4.3.)

- In every configuration γ_i with $i \in \{\frac{m}{2} + 1, \ldots, m\}$, for every process p_j with $j \in \{0, \ldots, \mathcal{D} - i + \frac{m}{2} - 1\}$, $p_j.clock = i \bmod m$, and for every process p_k with $k \in \{\mathcal{D} - i + \frac{m}{2}, \ldots, \mathcal{D}\}$, $p_k.clock = i - \frac{m}{2}$.

In particular, in γ_m, for every process p_j with $j \in \{0, \ldots, X-1\}$, $p_j.clock = 0$, and for every process p_k with $k \in \{X, \ldots, \mathcal{D}\}$, $p_k.clock = \frac{m}{2}$, i.e., $\gamma_m = \gamma_0$.

(See Configurations γ_5 to γ_8 in Figure 4.3.)

Hence, $(\gamma_0 \cdots \gamma_{m-1})^\omega$ is an infinite execution of Algorithm Unison which never converges and we can conclude with the following theorem.

Theorem 4.13   *For every $X \in \{1, \ldots, \mathcal{D}-1\}$, for every $m = 2(\mathcal{D}-X)$ (i.e., for every even number m such that $2 \leq m \leq 2\mathcal{D}-2$), there exists a synchronous execution of Algorithm Unison on a line graph of diameter $\mathcal{D} > 1$ that never converges.*

Table 4.2: A fragment of execution that does not converge with $\mathcal{D} = 5$, $X = 1$, and $m = 2(\mathcal{D} - X) = 8$

	p_0	p_1	p_2	p_3	p_4	p_5
γ_0	0	4	4	4	4	4
γ_1	1	1	5	5	5	5
γ_2	2	2	2	6	6	6
γ_3	3	3	3	3	7	7
γ_4	4	4	4	4	4	0
γ_5	5	5	5	5	1	1
γ_6	6	6	6	2	2	2
γ_7	7	7	3	3	3	3
γ_8	0	4	4	4	4	4

4.4   RELATED WORK

The self-stabilizing synchronous unison problem has been studied, assuming bounded local memories, in particular topologies, such as rings [HL98] and trees [NV01]. However, Gouda and Herman [GH90] tackled the problem in anonymous synchronous systems of arbitrary connected topology, yet considering unbounded clocks. Algorithm Unison, the solution studied in this chapter (originally proposed in [ADG91]), works under the same settings, but implementing bounded clocks. Nevertheless, there exists a self-stabilizing algorithm that achieves better performances than Algorithm Unison w.r.t. both time and space complexity. Indeed, Boulinier et al. show in [BPV08] that any self-stabilizing algorithm for the asynchronous variant of the unison problem[1] written in the atomic-state model is actually self-stabilizing for the syn-

---

[1]Recall that the safety property of the asynchronous unison requires the difference between every two neighboring clocks to be always at most one increment.

chronous unison problem when the daemon is synchronous. Based on this result, they in particular study the performance of the asynchronous unison algorithm they proposed in [BPV04] under the synchronous daemon. This latter algorithm stabilizes in anonymous tree-shaped synchronous networks to the synchronous unison within at most $2\mathcal{D}$ steps for any period $m \geq 3$ and without any extra state, hence using a constant number bits per process, while Algorithm Unison stabilizes in the worst case in $3\mathcal{D} - 2$ steps and requires $\Theta(\mathcal{D}) = \Theta(H)$ bits per process, where H is the height of the tree. They also propose a new algorithm that stabilizes in any anonymous connected synchronous network to the synchronous unison within at most $2\mathcal{D}$ steps for any period $m \geq 2$ using $m + \mathcal{D}$ states per process, i.e., $O(\log(m + \mathcal{D}))$ bits per process.

The first self-stabilizing asynchronous unison for general connected graphs was proposed by Couvreur et al. [CFG92].[2] It uses at least n^2 states per process, where n is the number of processes. However, no complexity analysis was given. Another solution which stabilizes in $O(n)$ rounds has been proposed by Boulinier et al. in [BPV04] using $m + \alpha$ states per process, where the period m should satisfy $m > C_G$ and α is a parameter that should satisfy $\alpha \geq T_G - 2$. C_G is the *cyclomatic characteristic* of the network G, i.e., the length of the shortest maximal cycle of a cycle basis of G if G is cyclic, and 2 if G is a tree. T_G is the length of the longest chordless cycle in a graph G. Boulinier also proposed in his Ph.D. thesis [Bou07] a parametric solution which generalizes both the solutions of [CFG92] and [BPV04]. In particular, the complexity analysis of this latter algorithm reveals an upper bound in $O(\mathcal{D}.n)$ rounds on the stabilization time of the Couvreur et al.'s algorithm.

Tzeng et al. [TJH10] studied a problem referred to as *phase synchronization*, also called *barrier synchronization* in the literature. This problem is weaker that the synchronous unison, but stronger than the asynchronous one. Indeed, its safety imposes that any legitimate configuration contains at most two consecutive clock values. They proposed a self-stabilizing solution for arbitrary connected rooted networks, assuming a distributed unfair daemon, that stabilizes in $O(n^2)$ rounds and requires $O(\Delta \cdot m)$ states per process, where m is the period and Δ the network degree. Finally, Johnen et al. investigated the self-stabilizing asynchronous unison in oriented trees in [JADT02]. They propose a space optimal solution which uses only 1 bit per process. However, as the period of their solution is $m = 2$, the problem they solve is actually the *phase synchronization* problem. Their algorithm stabilizes in $O(H)$ rounds, where H is the height of the tree network.

---

[2]This algorithm is shown assuming a central unfair daemon in [CFG92], but the parametric construction given in [Bou07] actually proves its self-stabilization under the distribute unfair daemon.

CHAPTER 5

BFS Spanning Tree Under a Distributed Unfair Daemon

In this chapter, we focus on the construction of *(spanning) distributed structures*. Various kinds of distributed structure constructions have been studied in the self-stabilizing literature, e.g., *minimal dominating sets* [KM06], *minimum weakly connected dominating sets* [KK07], *maximal independent sets* [YH15, HHJS03], *k-Hop Dominating Sets* [TK15, DLD+13, DDH+16], and *spanning trees* [CYH91, CD94, CDV09b, CRV11]. Notably, even though not mandatory, almost all of these constructions achieve *silence*.

Among those structures, spanning trees are of particular interest. Indeed, spanning trees are often involved in the design of *routing* [GHIJ14] and *broadcasting* tasks [BDPV99a], for example. Moreover, (silent) self-stabilizing spanning tree constructions are widely used as a basic building blocks of more complex self-stabilizing solutions. Indeed, *composition* is a popular way to design self-stabilizing algorithms [Tel01] since it allows to simplify both the design and the proofs. Various composition techniques have been introduced so far, e.g., *collateral composition* [GH91],[1] *fair composition* [Dol00], *cross-over composition* [BGJ01], and *conditional composition* [DGPV01]; and many self-stabilizing algorithms are actually made as a composition of a silent spanning tree algorithm and another algorithm designed for tree topologies, e.g., [KC99, DLD+13, BFP14, FYHY14, DDH+16].

Numerous self-stabilizing spanning tree constructions have been studied until now. For example, the spanning tree may be arbitrary [CYH91], *depth-first* [CD94], *breadth-first* [CDV09b, CRV11], *shortest-path* [GHIJ14], or *minimum* [BPRT16]. We focus here the construction of a Breadth-First Search (BFS) spanning tree in a rooted connected network, i.e., a spanning tree in which the distance (in terms of hops) from any node to the root is minimum.

5.1 THE PROBLEM

We consider the network $G = (V, E)$ is of arbitrary *connected* topology. Moreover, we assume the network is *rooted*, i.e., one process, called the *root* and noted r, is distinguished from the others. Non-root processes are then fully anonymous. A rooted network is also said to be *semi-anonymous*. In rooted networks, the aim is to differenciate the local algorithm of the root from that of other processes. By extension, the distributed algorithm is then also said to be *semi-*

---

[1] n.b., a variant of the collateral composition, called *hierarchical collateral composition*, will be studied in Chapter 7.

anonymous. Notice also that rooted networks and fully-identified networks (a.k.a. ID-based networks) have essentially the same expressive power in the atomic-state model. Indeed, it is possible to emulate one in the other: following the ideas proposed in [Dol00], we can use the preorder ranking given by any self-stabilizing depth-first token circulation such as the one proposed in [HC93] to identify a rooted network, while a self-stabilizing leader election algorithm, e.g., [ACD+17], allows to distinguish a root in an identified network.

The goal here is to construct a *spanning tree*, i.e., a subgraph $T = (V_T, E_T)$ of G satisfying $V_T = V$, $E_T \subseteq E$, and T is a tree. This tree is required to be rooted at r, i.e., tree-edges are *oriented* toward r. More precisely, using an output variable $p.par$, each non-root process p should designate as its *parent* its unique neighbor which is on the path linking p to r in T.

Moreover, we require the spanning tree to be BFS, i.e., the length of the elementary path linking any process p to r in T should be equal to $\|p, r\|$, the distance from p to r in G.

The algorithm we propose below is silent. Hence, its goal is to reach a terminal configuration, where *par* variables define a BFS spanning tree. In the reasoning, we will use the subgraph induced by the *par* variables, defined as follows.

Definition 5.1   Let $\mathcal{T} = (V_\mathcal{T}, E_\mathcal{T})$, where $V_\mathcal{T} = V$ and $E_\mathcal{T} = \{\{p, q\} \in E : q \neq r \wedge q.par = p\}$.

The terminal configuration should satisfy the specification predicate *BFST* defined as the conjunction of the following two properties.

- $\mathcal{T}$ is a tree.

- For every process p, the distance from p to r in $\mathcal{T}$ is equal to $\|p, r\|$, i.e., the distance from p to r in G.

Notice that, since (by definition) $V_\mathcal{T} = V$ and $E_\mathcal{T} \subseteq E$, it is sufficient to show that $\mathcal{T}$ is a tree to establish that it is a spanning tree.

5.2   THE ALGORITHM

A simple silent algorithm that builds a BFS spanning tree has been proposed by Dolev et al. [DIM93] in the register model. However, this algorithm is implemented using unbounded process local memories.

The algorithm we propose here, called Algorithm BFS, is a straightforward variant of the Dolev et al.'s algorithm working in the atomic-state model, assuming a distributed unfair daemon, and using bounded process local memories. Its design is close to the one of the Dolev et al.'s variants proposed in [DJ16]. The code of Algorithm BFS is given in Algorithms 5.3 and 5.4

To achieve bounded process local memories, we assume that all processes know a common upper bound D on the network diameter $\mathcal{D}$. Then, we use the following variables.

- Every process p maintains, using Action *CD*, a variable $p.d$, whose domain is $\{0, \ldots, D\}$.

Algorithm 5.3 Algorithm BFS, code for the root process r

Inputs:

$r.\mathcal{N}$: the set of r's neighbors
D : an integer such that $D \geq \mathcal{D}$

Variable:

$r.d \in \{0, \ldots, D\}$: the distance of r

Action:

CD :: $r.d \neq 0 \rightarrow r.d$ 0

Algorithm 5.4 Algorithm BFS, code for any non-root process p.

Inputs:

$p.\mathcal{N}$: the set of p's neighbors
D : an integer such that $D \geq \mathcal{D}$

Variables:

$p.d \in \{0, \ldots, D\}$: the distance of p
$p.par \in p.\mathcal{N}$: the parent pointer of p

Macro:

$Dist(p)$ $=$ $\min(\{q.d : q \in p.\mathcal{N}\} \cup \{D - 1\}) + 1$

Predicate:

$DistOK(p)$ $\overset{\text{def}}{=}$ $p.d - 1 = \min\{q.d : q \in p.\mathcal{N}\}$

Actions:

CD :: $p.d \neq Dist(p)$ $\rightarrow$ $p.d \leftarrow Dist(p)$
CP :: $DistOK(p) \wedge p.par.d \neq p.d - 1$ $\rightarrow$ $p.par$ $q \in p.\mathcal{N}$ s.t. $q.d = p.d - 1$

- Moreover, if p is a non-root process, then p additionally maintains, using Action CP, a parent pointer $p.par$, whose domain is $p.\mathcal{N}$.

An example of synchronous execution of Algorithm BFS is given in Figure 5.1. Processes compute, in their variable d, their distance to the root. So, r simply forces the value of $r.d$ to be 0, see Action CD in Algorithm 5.3 and step $(i) \mapsto (ii)$. Then, distance variables are corrected step by step as follows. Every non-root process p maintains $p.d$ to be the minimum value between

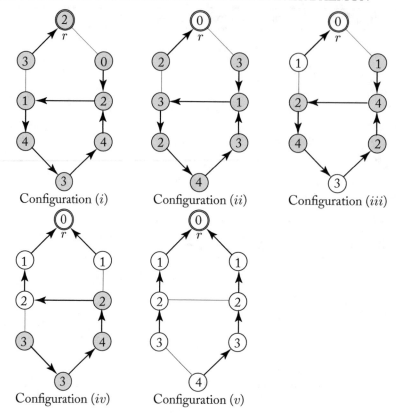

Figure 5.1: Example of synchronous execution of Algorithm BFS, with $D = \mathcal{D} = 4$: the double circled node is the root, the arrow from node p to node q indicates that p designates q as its parent using $p.par$, values of variable d are given inside the nodes, enabled nodes are filled in gray.

D and the values of the d variables of all its neighbors incremented by 1, see Action CD in Algorithm 5.4.

In parallel, each non-root process p chooses as parent a neighbor q such that $q.d = p.d - 1$, if any and whenever $p.d$ is locally correct (formally, whenever $DistOk(p)$ holds), see Action CP in Algorithm 5.4. Remark that a non-root process may have several processes candidate to be its parent, see, for example, the bottom node in Configuration (v) of Figure 5.1. We do not impose any choice in that case. In that sense, the algorithm is *nondeterministic*. Now, one can easily determine the choice of the parent using any local order, e.g., based on channel numbers.

First of all, it is important to note that Actions *CD* and *CP* are *locally mutually exclusive*, as proven below.

Lemma 5.2 *For every non-root process p, there is no configuration where both Action CD and Action CP are enabled at p.*

Proof. Assume, by contradiction, that Actions *CD* and *CP* are both enabled at some non-root process p in a given configuration γ. Then, in γ we have both $p.d \neq \min(\{q.d : q \in p.\mathcal{N}\} \cup \{D - 1\}) + 1$ (see the guard of Action *CD*) and $p.d - 1 = \min\{q.d : q \in p.\mathcal{N}\}$ (see the guard of Action *CP*). So, $p.d \neq \min(\{p.d - 1, D - 1\}) + 1$. Now, by definition, $p.d \leq D$. Thus, $p.d \neq p.d$, a contradiction. $\qquad\square$

5.3 PROOF OF SELF-STABILIZATION AND SILENCE

Recall that we assume a distributed unfair daemon. In the following proofs, we intensively use the following well-known properties on distances.

Property 5.3 Let p be any process.

- For every neighbor q of p, we have $\|q, r\| \in \{\|p, r\| - 1, \|p, r\|, \|p, r\| + 1\}$.

- If $p \neq r$, then there exists a neighbor q of p such that $\|q, r\| = \|p, r\| - 1$.

5.3.1 PARTIAL CORRECTNESS

We first show that every terminal configuration is legitimate, i.e., every terminal configuration satisfies the predicate *BFST*. To that goal, we consider any terminal configuration γ_t of Algorithm BFS.

The first part of the proof consists in showing that d variables are correctly assigned in γ_t (Lemma 5.5). The preliminary technical result below (Lemma 5.4) states that the values of these variables are not underestimated in γ_t.

Lemma 5.4 *For every process p, we have $p.d \geq \|p, r\|$ in γ_t.*

Proof. Assume, by contradiction, that there exists a process p such that $p.d < \|p, r\|$ in γ_t. Let $p_{\min} \in \{p \in V : \gamma_t(p).d < \|p, r\| \wedge (\forall q \in V, \gamma_t(q).d < \|q, r\| \Rightarrow \gamma_t(q).d \geq \gamma_t(p).d)\}$, i.e., $p_{\min}$ is a process with the minimum underestimated distance in γ_t. First, since, by definition, $r.d \geq 0 = \|r, r\|$, we have $p_{\min} \neq r$. Then, by definition of $p_{\min}$, each of its neighbor q satisfies one of the following two conditions:

- $\gamma_t(q).d \geq \gamma_t(p_{\min}).d$, or

- $\gamma_t(q).d \geq \|q, r\|$.

In the former case, we immediately have $\gamma_t(p_{\min}).d < \gamma_t(q).d + 1$. In the latter case, $\gamma_t(p_{\min}).d < \|p_{\min}, r\| \leq \|q, r\| + 1 \leq \gamma_t(q).d + 1$. Finally, $\gamma_t(p_{\min}).d < \|p_{\min}, r\| \leq \mathcal{D} \leq D = (D-1) + 1$. Hence, overall $\gamma_t(p_{\min}).d < \min(\{q.d : q \in p.\mathcal{N}\} \cup \{D-1\}) + 1 = Dist(p)$ and, since $p_{\min} \neq r$, Action CD is enabled at $p_{\min}$ in γ_t, a contradiction. $\square$

Lemma 5.5 *For every process p, we have $p.d = \|p, r\|$ in γ_t.*

Proof. By induction on the distances.

Base Case: By definition, the root is the unique process at distance 0 from itself. Then, since γ_t is terminal, Action CD is disabled at r and so $r.d = 0 = \|r, r\|$ in γ_t.

Induction Hypothesis: Let $k \geq 0$. Assume that for every process p such that $\|p, r\| = k$, we have $p.d = \|p, r\|$ in γ_t.

Induction Step: Let q be any process such that $\|q, r\| = k + 1$. Since $k + 1 > 0$, $q \neq r$ and there exists a neighbor q' of q such that $\|q', r\| = \|q, r\| - 1 = k$. By induction hypothesis, $q'.d = k$ in γ_t. Then, for every neighbor q'' of q, we have $\|q'', r\| \in \{k, k+1, k+2\}$ and, by Lemma 5.4, we have $q''.d \geq k$ in γ_t. Finally, since $\mathcal{D} \geq \|q, r\| = k + 1$, we have $k \leq \mathcal{D} - 1 \leq D - 1$. Thus, $Dist(q) = \min(\{q''.d : q'' \in q.\mathcal{N}\} \cup \{D-1\}) + 1 = k + 1 = \|q, r\|$ in γ_t and since γ_t is terminal, $q.d = Dist(q) = \|q, r\|$ in γ_t.

$\square$

We now show that *par* variables are correctly assigned in γ_t. The guard of Action CP (for any non-root process) consists of the conjunction of two properties. We first show that the former property, $DistOk$, is true in γ_t, for every non-root process, see Lemma 5.6. Hence, the latter property is necessarily false at every non-root process in γ_t, since Action CP is disabled; see Corollary 5.7.

Lemma 5.6 *For every non-root process p, $DistOk(p)$ holds in γ_t.*

Proof. Let p be a non-root process. By definition, p has a neighbor q such that $\|q, r\| = \|p, r\| - 1$. Moreover, in γ_t, $p.d = \|p, r\|$ and for every neighbor q' of p we have $q'.d = \|q', r\| \in \{\|p, r\| - 1, \|p, r\|, \|p, r\| + 1\}$ with in particular $q.d = \|p, r\| - 1$, by Lemma 5.5. So in γ_t, $p.d - 1 = \|p, r\| - 1 = \min\{q.d : q \in p.\mathcal{N}\}$, i.e., $DistOk(p)$ holds in γ_t. $\square$

From the previous lemma and the fact that Action CP is disabled at every non-root process in γ_t, we can deduce the following corollary.

Corollary 5.7 *For every non-root process p, $p.par.d = p.d - 1$ in γ_t.*

Since variables are correctly assigned in γ_t, we can deduce that γ_t is legitimate; see the lemma below.

Lemma 5.8 *The predicate BFST holds in any terminal configuration γ_t.* (Partial Correctness)

Proof. We first show that $\mathcal{T}$ is a tree in γ_t by using the classical equivalence: "a graph of n nodes is a tree if and only if it contains $n-1$ edges and is acyclic" [HHM00].

$|E_\mathcal{T}| = n-1$: Since every non-root process (i.e., $n-1$ processes) designates one edge with its parent pointer, we have $|E_\mathcal{T}| \leq n-1$ in γ_t. Assume now, by the contradiction, that two non-root processes p and q designate the same edge in γ_t. Then, by Corollary 5.7, $p.d < q.d$ and $p.d > q.d$, a contradiction.

$\mathcal{T}$ **is acyclic:** Assume, by contradiction, that $\mathcal{T}$ is not acyclic in γ_t. Then, in γ_t, $\mathcal{T}$ contains an elementary cycle, say $p_0, \ldots, p_k, p_0$ such that $\forall i \in \{0, k-1\}$, $p_i.par = p_{i+1}$ and $p_k.par = p_0$. Since that r has no parent pointer, it is not involved into that cycle. By Corollary 5.7, $p_i.d > p_{i+1}.d, \forall i \in \{0, \ldots, k-1\}$ and, by transitivity, $p_0.d > p_k.d$. Now, since $p_k.par = p_0$, we also have $p_0.d < p_k.d$, by Corollary 5.7, a contradiction.

Hence, $\mathcal{T}$ is a tree.

We now show that $\mathcal{T}$ is *breadth-first*, i.e., the length of the path from any process p to r in $\mathcal{T}$ is equal to $\|p, r\|$, the distance from p to r in G. Let $\mathcal{P} = p_0, \ldots, p_k$, with $p_0 = p$ and $p_k = r$, be the unique path from p to r in the tree $\mathcal{T}$ in γ_t. By definition, in γ_t, $\forall i \in \{0, \ldots, k-1\}$, $p_i.par = p_{i+1}$ and, by Corollary 5.7, $p_i.d = p_{i+1}.d + 1$. By transitivity, we have $p_0.d = p_k.d + k$ in γ_t. Now, $p_k = r$, so $p_k.d = 0$ in γ_t, by Lemma 5.5. So, $p_0.d = p.d = k$ in γ_t, i.e., $p.d$ is equal to length of the path $\mathcal{P}$ in γ_t. Now, by Lemma 5.5 again, $p.d = \|p, r\|$ in γ_t. Hence, $k = \|p, r\|$ in γ_t, i.e., the length k of the path from p to r in $\mathcal{T}$ is equal to $\|p, r\|$. $\square$

5.3.2 TERMINATION

By definition of the algorithm, we have the following remark.

Remark 5.9 In any execution, r executes Action CD at most once.

Since $Dist(p) > 0$ for every non-root process p in any configuration (n.b., if a non-root process exists, then $D \geq 1$ since the network is connected), we have:

Remark 5.10 Let p be a non-root process. Assume that p executes Action CD at least once. After the first execution of CD by p, $p.d > 0$ forever.

In the following proof, we use the notion of *limit inferior* of an infinite sequence $x_0, \ldots, x_i, \ldots$, denoted by $\liminf_{i \to \infty} x_i$. Recall that $\liminf_{i \to \infty} x_i = \lim_{i \to \infty}(\inf_{j \geq i} x_j)$. Notice that, when the domain of each x_i is finite, the limit inferior corresponds to the minimum value among those that appear infinitely often in the sequence. The proof technique used below has been introduced in [DDL19].

Theorem 5.11   *Only a finite number of Actions CD are executed in any execution of Algorithm* BFS.

Proof. Let $e = \gamma_0 \gamma_1 \cdots$ be an execution. Assume, by the contradiction, that an infinite number of Actions CD are executed in e. Then, e is infinite.

Let $\lambda(p) = \liminf_{t \to \infty} \gamma_t(p).d$ be the *limit inferior* of the sequence of values $\gamma_0(p).d, \gamma_1(p).d, \ldots$ Notice that, for every process p, the domain of $p.d$ is $\{0, \ldots, D\}$, hence $\lambda(p)$ exists and $\lambda(p) \in \{0, \ldots, D\}$.

Let F be the subset of processes that execute Action CD *finitely* many times in e. Let $I = V \setminus F$ be the subset of processes that execute Action CD *infinitely often* in e.

Since e is infinite, $I \neq \emptyset$. Pick a process $p \in I$ such that $\lambda(p) = d$ is minimum. If $p = r$, then p can execute Action CD at most once (see Remark 5.9), so $p \notin I$, a contradiction.

Assume now that $p \neq r$. If $\lambda(p) = D$, then since D is the maximum value that $p.d$ can take, eventually $p.d = D$ forever, so again $p \notin I$, a contradiction. Hence, $0 < \lambda(p) < D$ (since after the first execution of Action CD by p, $p.d > 0$ forever; see Remark 5.10). Since p executes Action CD infinitely many times and $\lambda(p) = d$, we know that $p.d \leftarrow d$ by Action CD infinitely often, so $Dist(p) = d < D$ infinitely often. As the number of neighbors of p is finite, there is some neighbor q of p such that $q.d = d - 1$ infinitely often, and thus $\lambda(q) \leq d - 1$. Because of our choice of p, $q \notin I$, i.e., $q \in F$. So, eventually $q.d = d - 1$ forever. This implies that eventually $Dist(p) \leq d$ forever, which in turn implies that eventually $p.d \leq d$ forever (remember that p executes Action CD infinitely often). Now, since $\lambda(p) = d$, eventually $p.d = d$ forever, i.e., $p \in F$, that is $p \notin I$, a contradiction. $\square$

The number of executions of Action CP by non-root processes is directly related to the number of executions of Action CD. Indeed, if a non-root process p executes CP in $\gamma_i \mapsto \gamma_{i+1}$, then CP is continuously disabled at p from γ_{i+1}, unless one of its neighbors executes CD in $\gamma_j \mapsto \gamma_{j+1}$ with $j \geq i$. (Actually, the variables involved in the guard of CP are $p.par$, $p.d$, and the d variables of all its neighbors, and recall that if p executes CP in $\gamma_i \mapsto \gamma_{i+1}$, then CD is disabled at p in γ_i, by Lemma 5.2.) Hence, the fact that only a finite number of Actions CD are executed in any execution implies, in turn, that only a finite number of Actions CP are executed in any execution, and follows.

Corollary 5.12   *Every execution of Algorithm* BFS *is finite.* (Termination)

By Lemma 5.8 and Corollary 5.12, Theorem 5.13 follows.

Theorem 5.13   *If $D \geq \mathcal{D}$, then Algorithm* BFS *is silent and self-stabilizing for configuration predicate BFST (i.e., the BFS spanning tree construction specification) in every connected rooted network under the distributed unfair daemon.*

5.4   COMPLEXITY ANALYSIS

5.4.1   MEMORY REQUIREMENT

Every process p holds a variable $p.d$ whose domain is $\{0, \ldots, D\}$ with $D \geq \mathcal{D}$. Moreover, every non-root process q holds a variable whose domain is $q.\mathcal{N}$ with $|q.\mathcal{N}| = \delta_p \leq \Delta$ (Δ is the maximum degree of the network). So, the memory requirement of Algorithm BFS is in $\Theta(\log D + \log \delta_p)$ bits per non-root process p and in $\Theta(\log D)$ bits for the root (D is in $\Omega(\mathcal{D})$). Overall, the memory requirement of Algorithm BFS is in $O(\log D + \log \Delta)$ bits.

Notice that Johnen proposed a more space efficient self-stabilizing algorithm for computing a BFS spanning tree under a distributed unfair daemon [Joh97]: her solution is in $O(\log \Delta)$ bits per process. However, the proposed algorithm is not silent and its stabilization time is unknown until now.

We now consider the overhead in memory requirement of Algorithm BFS. In our model, a silent non self-stabilizing algorithm (i.e., assuming the algorithm starts from a predefined initial configuration) for computing a BFS spanning tree can be implemented using $\Theta(\log \Delta)$ bits per process (follow, for example, the ideas given in [BDLP08]). Hence, the overhead of BFS in terms of memory requirement is $O\left(\frac{\log D}{\log \Delta}\right)$.

5.4.2   TIME COMPLEXITY

Stabilization Time in Rounds

The proof consists first in showing that d variables are correctly evaluated within at most $\mathcal{D} + 1$ rounds (Corollary 5.15). This result is based on the technical Lemma 5.14. As a direct consequence of this result, we show in Lemma 5.16 that all Actions CD are disabled forever after at most $\mathcal{D} + 1$ rounds. Finally, one additional round may be necessary to make all Actions CP disabled (Lemma 5.17). Hence, we can conclude in Theorem 5.18 that the stabilization time of Algorithm BFS is at most $\mathcal{D} + 2$ rounds.

Lemma 5.14   *Let $k \geq 1$. After at most k rounds, every process p forever satisfies:*

- *if $\|p, r\| < k$, then $p.d = \|p, r\|$, and*

- *$p.d \geq k$ otherwise.*

Proof. By induction on k.

Base Case: Let $k = 1$. First, r is the unique process such that $\|r, r\| < 1$. As soon as $r.d = 0$, Action CD is disabled at r forever, and so $r.d = \|r, r\| = 0$ forever. Now, if $r.d \neq 0$, then Action CD is enabled at r. Hence, within at most one round, r executes $r.d \leftarrow 0$ by Action CD and we are done.

Then, let p be any non-root process. Since $Dist(p) > 0$ (by definition), if $p.d > 0$ in some configuration γ, then $p.d > 0$ forever from γ. Otherwise (i.e., $p.d = 0$) Action CD is enabled at p until p executes it. So, since Actions CD and CP are locally mutually exclusive (Lemma 5.2), p executes Action CD within at most one round in that case, and we are done by Remark 5.10.

Induction Hypothesis: Assume that the lemma holds for some value $k \geq 1$.

Induction Step: From the induction hypothesis, we need only to consider processes at distance at least k from the root.

Let p be a process such that $\|p, r\| = k$. First, since $\|p, r\| = k$, $k - 1 \leq \mathcal{D} - 1 \leq D - 1$. Then, since $\|p, r\| = k \geq 1$, $p \neq r$ and so p has a neighbor p' such that $\|p', r\| = k - 1$ that forever satisfies $p'.d = k - 1$ starting from last configuration of the kth round, i.e., the first configuration of the $k + 1^{th}$ round, by induction hypothesis. Moreover, every neighbor p'' of p satisfies $\|p'', r\| \in \{k - 1, k, k + 1\}$ and, still by induction hypothesis, forever satisfies $p''.d \geq k - 1$ starting from the first configuration of the $k + 1^{th}$ round. Hence, starting from the first configuration of the $k + 1^{th}$ round, $\min(\{p''.d : p'' \in p.\mathcal{N}\} \cup \{D - 1\}) = k - 1$, i.e., $Dist(p) = k$, forever. Consequently, if $p.d = k$ at the beginning of the $k + 1^{th}$ round, then $p.d = k$ forever. Otherwise, Action CD is enabled at p until p executes it. So, since Actions CD and CP are locally mutually exclusive (Lemma 5.2), before the end of the $k + 1^{th}$ round, p executes $p.d \leftarrow k$ by Action CD, and then forever satisfies $p.d = k = \|p, r\|$.

Let q be a process such that $\|q, r\| \geq k + 1$. Since $\|q, r\| > k$, $k \leq \mathcal{D} - 1 \leq D - 1$. By definition, every neighbor of q is at distance at least k from r. So, by induction hypothesis, every neighbor q' of q satisfies $q'.d \geq k$ forever at the beginning of the $k + 1^{th}$ round. That is to say, $\min_{q' \in q.\mathcal{N}} q'.d \geq k$ holds forever at the beginning of the $k + 1^{th}$ round. Moreover, $k \leq D - 1$. So, $\min(\{q'.d : q' \in q.\mathcal{N}\} \cup \{D - 1\}) \geq k$, i.e., $Dist(q) \geq k + 1$, forever at the beginning of the $k + 1^{th}$ round. Hence, if $q.d \geq k + 1$ at the beginning of the $k + 1^{th}$ round, then $q.d \geq k + 1$ forever. Otherwise, Action CD is enabled at q until q executes it. So, since Actions CD and CP are locally mutually exclusive (Lemma 5.2), before the end of the $k + 1^{th}$ round, q sets $q.d$ to $Dist(q) \geq k + 1$, by Action CD, and then forever satisfies $q.d \geq k + 1$.

$\square$

Let $k = \mathcal{D} + 1$. Since every process p satisfies $\|p, r\| < k = \mathcal{D} + 1$, we obtain the following corollary from the previous lemma.

Corollary 5.15 *After at most $\mathcal{D} + 1$ rounds, for every process p we have $p.d = \|p, r\|$ forever.*

Lemma 5.16 *After at most $\mathcal{D} + 1$ rounds, Action CD is disabled forever at every process.*

Proof. Let γ be the first configuration from which $p.d = \|p, r\|$ forever, for every process p. Configuration γ appears within at most $\mathcal{D} + 1$ rounds in the execution, by Corollary 5.15. Let now consider any process p. If $p = r$, then $p.d = \|p, r\| = 0$ forever from γ, and so Action CD is disabled at p forever from γ. Otherwise, $\|p, r\| \leq \mathcal{D} \leq D$ and for every neighbor q of p, we have $\|q, r\| \in \{\|p, r\| - 1, \|p, r\|, \|p, r\| + 1\}$. Moreover, from γ, $p.d$ and every $q.d$ are constant forever, and $q.d \in \{p.d - 1, p.d, p.d + 1\}$, with in particular at least one neighbor q' satisfying, $q'.d = p.d - 1 \leq D - 1$. Hence, $\min(\{q.d : q \in p.\mathcal{N}\} \cup \{D - 1\}) = p.d - 1$, i.e., $Dist(p) = p.d$, forever from γ. Thus, Action CD is disabled forever at p from γ, and we are done. $\qquad\square$

Lemma 5.17   *After at most $\mathcal{D} + 2$ rounds, Action CP is disabled forever at every process.*

Proof. From Lemma 5.16 and the code of Action CP, we can deduce that, at the beginning of the $\mathcal{D} + 2^{th}$ round, the value $p.par$ for every non-root process p only depends on constant values. Thus, if Action CP at p, which computes the value of $p.par$, is disabled, it is disabled forever. Otherwise, Action CP is enabled at p until p executes it. Now, since all Actions CD are disabled (Lemma 5.16), p executes Action CP within at most one round in this latter case. Moreover, by definition, p has a neighbor q such that $\|q, r\| = \|p, r\| - 1$, and by Corollary 5.15 again, $q.d = p.d - 1$ forever at the beginning of the $\mathcal{D} + 2^{th}$ round. Thus, the execution of CP by p makes its guard false forever, and we are done. $\qquad\square$

By Lemmas 5.16 and 5.17, Theorem 5.18 follows.

Theorem 5.18   *The stabilization time of Algorithm BFS is at most $\mathcal{D} + 2$ rounds.*

We now show that the upper bound given in the previous theorem is reachable. Our reasoning is illustrated with Figure 5.2. Consider a connected network consisting of a line of $\mathcal{D} + 2$ processes $p_0 = r, \ldots, p_{\mathcal{D}+1}$ and an additional edge linking $p_{\mathcal{D}-1}$ and $p_{\mathcal{D}+1}$. Initially, variables are set as follows:

- for every process p_i ($i \in \{0, \ldots, \mathcal{D} + 1\}$), $p_i.d = D$, and

- for every non-root process p_i ($i \in \{1, \ldots, \mathcal{D} + 1\}$), $p_i.par = p_{i-1}$.

Assume now that $D > \mathcal{D}$ and the daemon is synchronous. Recall that, in that case, each round lasts exactly one step. Actually, as we will see, the synchronous execution will be almost sequential since it will contain only one configuration where more than one process is enabled.

The execution can be split into the following three phases.

1. At each round $i \in \{1, \ldots, \mathcal{D}\}$, only p_{i-1} executes: it definitely sets $p_{i-1}.d$ to $i - 1$ using Action CD.

2. At round $\mathcal{D} + 1$, both $p_{\mathcal{D}}$ and $p_{\mathcal{D}+1}$ definitely set their variable d to $\mathcal{D}$ using Action CD.

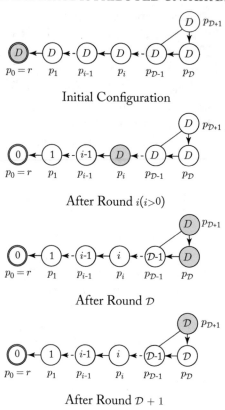

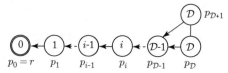

Figure 5.2: Worst-case (synchronous) execution of Algorithm BFS with $D > \mathcal{D}$: the double circled node is the root, the arrow from node p to node q indicates that p designates q as its parent using $p.par$, values of variable d are given inside the nodes, enabled nodes are filled in gray.

3. At round $\mathcal{D} + 2$, only $p_{\mathcal{D}+1}$ executes: it definitely sets $p_{\mathcal{D}+1}.par$ to $p_{\mathcal{D}-1}$ using Action CP.

Thus, this execution lasts exactly $\mathcal{D} + 2$ rounds.

If we now consider the same initial configuration but assume $D = \mathcal{D}$, then the execution under the synchronous daemon is fully sequentially since it consists of Phases 1 and 3 of the previous execution. In this case, we obtain an execution that lasts exactly $\mathcal{D} + 1$ rounds. Hence, Theorem 5.19 follows.

Theorem 5.19 *If $D > \mathcal{D}$ (resp. $D = \mathcal{D}$), then there are connected rooted networks for which there exists an execution of BFS that converges in $\mathcal{D} + 2$ rounds (resp. $\mathcal{D} + 1$ rounds).*

Stabilization Time in Moves/Steps

The fact that local memories are bounded is not only relevant from the space complexity point of view. Indeed, as we shall see, it is also important regarding step/move complexity issues.

Recall that the Dolev et al.'s Algorithm [DIM93] has been implemented in the register model using unbounded process local memories, precisely the distance variable is an unbounded integer. In this chapter, we have proposed a straightforward adaptation of the Dolev et al.'s algorithm, called Algorithm BFS, designed for the atomic-state model, assuming a distributed unfair daemon, and using bounded process local memories. Actually, two other variants of the Dolev et al.'s Algorithm have been previously proposed in [DJ16] in the atomic-state model, assuming a distributed unfair daemon. The former, called here Algorithm UB, is implemented using *unbounded* process local memories, while the latter, called here Algorithm B, is implemented using *bounded* process local memories.

The designs of BFS, UB, and B are closed. However, Algorithm UB has a step/move complexity that cannot be bounded. Precisely, it is shown in [DJ16] that there exists a graph L—actually a line of 5 processes where the root is located at one of the two extremities—and an execution e of UB in L such that e converges in more than $f(L)$ steps, where f is any function mapping graphs to integers. Now, in contrast, we show in Theorem 5.20 (this theorem first appeared in [DJ16]) that any self-stabilizing algorithm that uses bounded local process memories and works assuming an unfair daemon has a step complexity (and so, a move complexity too) which is inherently bounded.

The theorem below exhibits a trivial upper bound on the stabilization time in steps of every self-stabilizing algorithm working under an unfair daemon.

Theorem 5.20 *Let A be any self-stabilizing algorithm under an unfair daemon,[2] the stabilization time of A is less than or equal to $\prod_{p \in V} |S_p| - 1$ steps, where S_p is the set of possible states of p, for every process p.*

Proof. First, the number of possible configurations of A is $\prod_{p \in V} |S_p|$. Let e be any execution of A. A being self-stabilizing, e contains a maximal prefix of finite size $e' = \gamma_0 \gamma_1 \cdots \gamma_s$ made of illegitimate configurations only. Let e'' such that $e = e'e''$.

---

[2]The daemon may be central or distributed.

Assume, by contradiction, that $\exists k, \ell$ such that $0 \le k < \ell \le s$ and $\gamma_k = \gamma_\ell$. Then, $(\gamma_k \cdots \gamma_{\ell-1})^\omega$ is an infinite execution of A under the unfair daemon that never converges to a legitimate configuration. So, A is not self-stabilizing under an unfair daemon, a contradiction.

Hence, all configurations of e' are distinct. Moreover, $|e''| \ge 1$ and e' and e'' have no common configuration (cf. the closure property of self-stabilization in Definition 2.1, page 17). Hence, e' contains at most $\prod_{p \in V} |S_p| - 1$ configurations, and so the execution reaches a legitimate configuration within at most $\prod_{p \in V} |S_p| - 1$ steps. □

The previous theorem is useless when considering algorithms where at least one variable as an infinite domain, e.g., an integer. However, for Algorithm BFS, the theorem claims that its stabilization time is less than or equal to $(\Delta.(D + 1))^{n-1}.(D + 1) - 1$ steps. This upper bound may appear to be overestimated at the first glance. However, one can adapt the worst case of the silent BFS algorithm exhibited in [DJ16] (precisely, an execution in a particular class of graphs which lasts $\Omega(2^D)$ steps) to show that Algorithm BFS has also an exponential step/move complexity in the worst case.

Finally, notice that there exists a silent self-stabilizing BFS spanning tree algorithm in the literature that is polynomial in steps: the algorithm proposed by Cournier et al. [CRV11] converges in $O(n^6)$ steps and $O(D^2)$ rounds. Actually, this latter algorithm is said to be *fully polynomial*, i.e., its round complexity is polynomial on the network diameter and its step complexity is polynomial on the network size.

CHAPTER 6

Dijkstra's Token Ring

In this chapter we study the first self-stabilizing algorithm proposed by Dijkstra in its two pioneer papers [Dij73, Dij74]. We should notice that the proof of self-stabilization of this algorithm was only sketched in the technical report [Dij73] and was simply omitted in the published paper [Dij74]:

"For brevity's sake most of the heuristics that led me to find them, together with the proofs that they satisfy the requirements, have been omitted, [...]"

However, the correctness of this algorithm have been addressed later in several papers, e.g., [KRS99, FHP05].

6.1 THE PROBLEM

The *token ring* problem consists in implementing the infinite circulation of a single token in a *ring* network. In arbitrary networks, this problem is more generally referred to as *the token circulation problem*. In our model, the fact that a process p holds a token is modeled by a predicate noted $Token(p)$ that involves variables of p and its neighbors. An execution $e = \gamma_0 \cdots \gamma_i \cdots$ satisfies the specification of the token circulation if the predicate $TC(e)$ holds, where $TC(e)$ is defined by the conjunction of the following two properties.

Safety: In each configuration, there is at most one token holder: $\forall i \geq 0, \forall p, q \in V, Token(p) \wedge Token(q)$ holds in $\gamma_i \Rightarrow p = q$.

Liveness: Each process holds the token infinitely often: $\forall i \geq 0, \forall p \in V, \exists j \geq i, Token(p)$ in γ_j.

The network is assumed to be a ring, i.e., a graph whose vertices are arranged as an elementary cycle. Nodes of the ring are denoted by $p_0, \ldots, p_{n-1}$ with $n \geq 3$ (n.b., a ring has at least 3 nodes): each process p_x (with $x \in \{0, \ldots, n-1\}$) has two neighbors p_{x-1} and p_{x+1} (subscripts are understood modulo n). The ring is assumed to be *rooted* and *oriented*. Recall that "rooted" means that one process, called the *root* and noted here p_0, is distinguished among others (non-root processes are then fully anonymous, subscripts are just used for reasoning). By "oriented" we mean that every process p_x differentiates its two neighbors as a *predecessor* and a *successor*. Moreover, the orientation is consistent in the sense that the successor of the predecessor of p_x is p_x itself, for every process p_x. We consider, without loss of generality, a clockwise orientation,

---

Algorithm 6.5 Algorithm Token, code for the root p_0

Inputs:

$p_0.Pred$	:	the predecessor of p_0 in the ring
K	:	a positive integer

Variable:

$p_0.v \in \{0, \dots, K-1\}$

Predicate:

$Token(p_0) \overset{\text{def}}{=} p_0.v = p_0.Pred.v$

Action:

$T \quad :: \quad Token(p_0) \quad \rightarrow \quad p_0.v \leftarrow (p_0.v + 1) \bmod K$

---

i.e., p_{x-1} is the predecessor of p_x and p_{x+1} is its successor. In the local algorithm of p_x (for every $x \in \{0, \dots, n-1\}$), the local label designating the predecessor p_{x-1} of p_x will be denoted by $p_x.Pred$.

The self-stabilizing token ring algorithm we present here aims at working under a distributed unfair daemon (if a given parameter K is correctly assigned, as we shall see later). Note that, in this case, assuming the system is not fully anonymous is mandatory, since otherwise the problem cannot be solved by a deterministic algorithm. Indeed, following a reasoning similar to the proof of Theorem 3.1 (page 23), there are possible initial symmetric configurations from which no deterministic algorithm is able to break the initial symmetry if the execution is synchronous; and so no unique token holder can be ever distinguished in any configuration of such an execution.

6.2   THE ALGORITHM

The algorithm we present now is the first self-stabilizing algorithm proposed by Dijkstra [Dij73, Dij74] and is referred to as Algorithm Token in the sequel. As explained before, it is semi-anonymous: the code for the root is given in Algorithm 6.5, the code for the other processes is given in Algorithm 6.6. In this algorithm, each process p_x maintains a single variable $p_x.v$ whose domain is $\{0, \dots, K-1\}$, where K is a positive integer whose value will be discussed later. Each process p_x determines if it holds a token, using predicate $Token(p_x)$, by comparing its variable to that of its predecessor. When holding a token, p_x tries to pass it to its successor by executing action T.

Recall that to circumvent the impossibility of breaking symmetries (e.g., when all variables have the same initial value), the action of the root should be different from that of non-root

---

Algorithm 6.6 Algorithm Token, code for each non-root process p_x with $x \in \{1, \ldots, n-1\}$

Inputs:

$p_x.Pred$:   the predecessor of p_x in the ring

K :   a positive integer

Variable:

$p_x.v \in \{0, \ldots, K-1\}$

Predicate:

$Token(p_x) \overset{\text{def}}{=} p_x.v \neq p_x.Pred.v$

Action:

$T \quad :: \quad Token(p_x) \quad \rightarrow \quad p_x.v \leftarrow p_x.Pred.v$

---

processes: the root holds a token (i.e., $Token(p_0)$ is true) if its value is equal to that of its predecessor p_{n-1}, while a non-root process p_x holds a token (i.e., $Token(p_x)$ is true) if its value is different from that of its predecessor p_{x-1}. Notice that this asymmetry also ensures that there is no configuration without token (as shown in Lemma 6.1). Therefore, the set of legitimate configurations will be simply defined as the set of configurations where there is exactly one process satisfying its predicate Token (see Definition 6.3).

To (try to) pass the token, a token holder p_x should, in particular, falsify the predicate $Token(p_x)$ when executing T. It consists for the root in incrementing $p_0.v$ modulo K, while a non-root process p_x simply duplicates in $p_x.v$ the value of $p_{x-1}.v$, i.e., the tokens progress clockwise in the ring. It is important to note that after some process p_x executes T, either its successor becomes the token holder (like in step $(i) \mapsto (ii)$ of Figure 6.1), or the token disappears (like in step $(ii) \mapsto (iii)$ of Figure 6.1); however, recall that there is always at least one token.

An example of convergence of Algorithm Token is presented in Figure 6.1. The main ideas behind this convergence phenomenon (in particular the connection with the value of K) are detailed in the next sections.

A fragment of execution starting from a legitimate configuration is given in Figure 6.2.

Initially [Dij73, Dij74], Dijkstra presented this algorithm assuming a central unfair daemon and $K \geq n$ (even if he already conjectured that the solution still self-stabilizes when $K = n - 1$). Fokkink et al. [FHP05] propose a proof for $K \geq n - 1$ but still assuming a central unfair daemon. The correctness has been studied in several other papers and books, e.g., [KRS99, Tel01]. In particular, Gerard Tel [Tel01] shows the self-stabilization of Token assuming $K \geq n$ and a distributed unfair daemon.

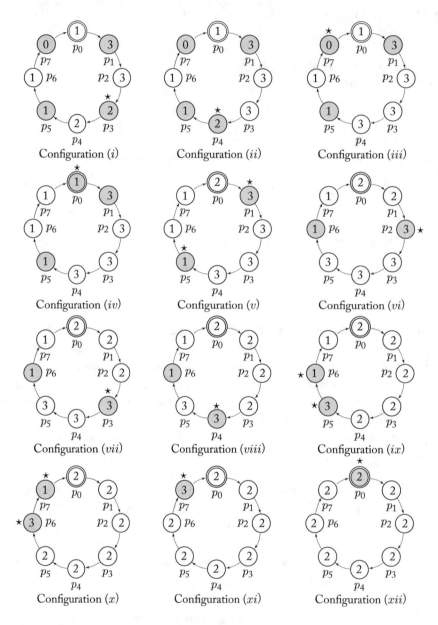

Figure 6.1: Example of convergence of Algorithm Token: the double-circled node is the root, the arrow from node p_x to node p_{x+1} indicates that p_x is the predecessor of p_{x+1}, values of variable v are given inside the nodes, enabled nodes are filled in gray, and nodes activated in the next step are marked with a star.

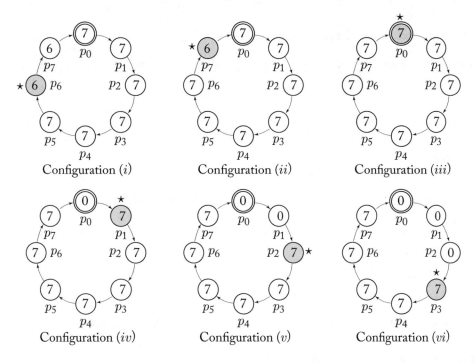

Figure 6.2: Fragment of execution of Algorithm Token, with $K = n = 8$, starting from a legitimate configuration.

We propose in Section 6.3 below to study the correctness and the complexity of Token assuming $K \geq n$ and a distributed unfair daemon. The correctness proof we propose is inspired by the one given in [Tel01]. Interestingly, we also show that the result of Fokkink et al. [FHP05] cannot be extended to the distributed unfair daemon: for any $K < n$ (in particular in the case $K = n - 1$), there are infinite distributed non-sequential executions that do not self-stabilize.

In Section 6.4, we extend the result of Fokkink et al. [FHP05] by assuming a locally central unfair daemon. We also show that the bound $K = n - 1$ is tight in this case: for any $K < n - 1$, there are sequential executions that do not self-stabilize.

6.3   STUDY ASSUMING $K \geq n$ AND A DISTRIBUTED UNFAIR DAEMON

6.3.1   PROOF OF SELF-STABILIZATION

We now show the self-stabilization of Algorithm Token in any oriented rooted ring of $n \geq 3$ processes assuming a distributed unfair daemon and $K \geq n$.

Absence of Deadlock

First, using the definition of *Token*, we have the following.

Lemma 6.1   *In every configuration* γ, *there exists at least one process* p_x *with* $x \in \{0, \dots, n-1\}$ *such that Token(p_x) holds in* γ.

Proof. Assume, by contradiction, that there exists a configuration γ where $\neg Token(p_x)$ holds, for every $x \in \{0, \dots, n-1\}$. Then, for every $x \in \{1, \dots, n-1\}$ (i.e., for every non-root process), we have $p_x.v = p_x.Pred.v = p_{x-1}.v$, by definition of *Token*(p_x). Then, by transitivity, we have $p_{n-1}.v = p_0.v$. Since $p_0.Pred = p_{n-1}$, *Token*(p_0) holds in γ, a contradiction.   □

Since every process satisfying *Token* is enabled (for Action T), we have the following.

Corollary 6.2   *No configuration of* Token *is terminal.*

Closure and Correctness

We define the set of legitimate configurations as follows.

Definition 6.3   Let $\mathcal{L}$ be the set of configurations where there is a unique process p_x with $x \in \{0, \dots, n-1\}$ satisfying *Token*(p_x). In the following, we refer to $\mathcal{L}$ as the set of legitimate configurations of Algorithm Token.

Since the configuration where every process satisfies $p_x.v = 0$ exists, independently of the choice of K, and is legitimate, we have the following.

Remark 6.4 $\mathcal{L} \neq \emptyset$.

The next lemma establishes the closure and correctness properties (see Definition 2.1, page 17).

Lemma 6.5 $\mathcal{L}$ *is closed and for every execution* e *in* $\mathcal{E}(\mathcal{L})$ *(i.e., for every execution* e *initiated in* $\mathcal{L}$), $TC(e)$ *holds.* (Closure and Correctness)

Proof. Let $\gamma_i \mapsto \gamma_{i+1}$ be a step such that $\gamma_i \in \mathcal{L}$. By definition, there is exactly one enabled process in γ_i, say p_x. So, p_x is the only process that moves in $\gamma_i \mapsto \gamma_{i+1}$, and (*) for every $y \in \{0, \dots, n-1\} \setminus \{x\}$, $\gamma_{i+1}(p_y).v = \gamma_i(p_y).v$.

Property (*) implies that $\neg Token(p_y)$ still holds in γ_{i+1}, for every $y \in \{0, \dots, n-1\} \setminus \{x, x+1\}$ (because *Token*(p_y) depends on the state of p_y and that of its predecessor).

Another consequence of (*) is that p_x falsifies $Token(p_x)$ by executing Action T in $\gamma_i \mapsto \gamma_{i+1}$: *Token*($p_x$) does not hold in γ_{i+1}.

Hence, p_{x+1} is necessarily the unique process that satisfies the predicate *Token* in γ_{i+1}, by Lemma 6.1: γ_{i+1} is legitimate (i.e., $\mathcal{L}$ is closed) and the unique token moves from a p_x to its successor in $\gamma_i \mapsto \gamma_{i+1}$, i.e., starting from a legitimate configuration, the unique token passes through all processes every n steps (i.e., $\forall e \in \mathcal{E}(\mathcal{L})$, $TC(e)$ holds).   □

Convergence

We now consider an arbitrary execution $e = \gamma_0 \cdots \gamma_i \cdots$ of Algorithm Token.

Since there always exists at least one token and since tokens move clockwise, we will show (see Corollary 6.9) that the root executes Action T infinitely often. To prove this result, we proceed by contradiction and consider the following potential function.

Definition 6.6 Let p_x be a process. We define the *local potential* of p_x as follows:

- $pot(p_x) = n - x$ if $x \neq 0 \land Token(p_x)$, i.e., if p_x is a non-root token holder;

- $pot(p_x) = 0$ otherwise.

Let $Pot = \Sigma_{y \in \{0,\dots,n-1\}} pot(p_y)$ be the *global potential* of the current configuration. Let $\gamma_i \mapsto \gamma_{i+1}$ be any step of e. We denote by $\Delta_{pot(p_x)}$ the difference between the value of $pot(p_x)$ in γ_{i+1} and the value of $pot(p_x)$ in γ_i.

Note that $\Delta_{pot(p_x)} \in \{x - n, 0, n - x\}$, e.g., in Step $(i) \mapsto (ii)$ of Figure 6.1, $\Delta_{pot(p_3)} = -5$, $\Delta_{pot(p_4)} = 4$, and $\Delta_{pot(p_5)} = 0$. Then, by definition we have the following.

Remark 6.7 In any configuration, we have $0 \leq Pot \leq \frac{n(n-1)}{2}$.

In Figure 6.3, we propose a configuration where $Pot = 0$. In the configuration given in Figure 6.4, $Pot = 12$. Finally, Pot is maximum in the configuration given in Figure 6.5: in this example, $Pot = 28$ and $n = 8$.

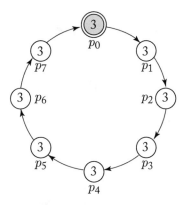

Figure 6.3: Example of configuration where $Pot = 0$.

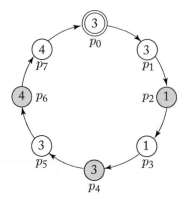

Figure 6.4: Example of configuration where *Pot* is positive (= 12).

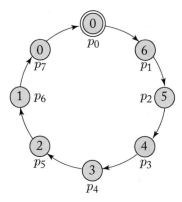

Figure 6.5: Example of worst-case configuration where $Pot = \frac{n(n-1)}{2} = 28$.

Lemma 6.8   *Let $\gamma_i \mapsto \gamma_{i+1}$ be any step of e. If $p_0 \notin Activated(\gamma_i, \gamma_{i+1})$ (i.e., the root p_0 does not move in $\gamma_i \mapsto \gamma_{i+1}$), then Pot > 0 in γ_i and Pot decreases in $\gamma_i \mapsto \gamma_{i+1}$.*

Proof. (The following proof is illustrated with Figure 6.1.)

First, since the daemon is proper, $Activated(\gamma_i, \gamma_{i+1}) \neq \emptyset$. Now, by hypothesis, $p_0 \notin Activated(\gamma_i, \gamma_{i+1})$. So, there is at least one non-root process p_x (with $x \in \{1 \ldots n-1\}$) such that $p_x \in Activated(\gamma_i, \gamma_{i+1})$. By definition of Algorithm Token, $Token(p_x)$ holds in γ_i. Hence, $Pot > 0$ in γ_i by Definition 6.6.

We now show that *Pot* decreases in $\gamma_i \mapsto \gamma_{i+1}$.

Claim I: *There exists a non-root process p_x such that $pot(p_x)$ decreases between γ_i and γ_{i+1}.*

Proof of the claim: The potential of a non-root process p_y decreases in $\gamma_i \mapsto \gamma_{i+1}$ if and only if p_y is enabled in γ_i but not in γ_{i+1}.

Let $p_x \in Activated(\gamma_i, \gamma_{i+1})$ such that x is minimum, e.g., p_3 in Step $(i) \mapsto (ii)$ of Figure 6.1. Since $p_0 \notin Activated(\gamma_i, \gamma_{i+1})$ (by hypothesis), p_x is non-root process. Moreover, $p_{x-1} \notin Activated(\gamma_i, \gamma_{i+1})$. By definition of Action T, p_x is enabled in γ_i but not in γ_{i+1}, i.e., $pot(p_x)$ decreases between γ_i and γ_{i+1}.

Consider now any process p_x such that $pot(p_x)$ increases between γ_i and γ_{i+1}, e.g., p_4 in Step $(i) \mapsto (ii)$ of Figure 6.1. Remark that p_x is disabled in γ_i but enabled in γ_{i+1}, in particular this means that p_{x-1} moves in $\gamma_i \mapsto \gamma_{i+1}$ (by definition of Action T).

Again, since $p_0 \notin Activated(\gamma_i, \gamma_{i+1})$ (by hypothesis), there is a non-root process p_y such that $1 \leq y < x$ such that $pot(p_y)$ decreases between γ_i and γ_{i+1}, i.e., p_y is enabled in γ_i but not in γ_{i+1}. Consider the maximum y subject to that condition. We call p_y the *witness of p_x* and we note $W(p_x) = p_y$, e.g., in Step $(ix) \mapsto (x)$ of Figure 6.1, the witness of p_7 is p_5. Remark that since $y < x$, $-\Delta_{pot(W(p_x))} = -\Delta_{pot(p_y)} > \Delta_{pot(p_x)}$, i.e., $pot(p_y)$ decreases more that $pot(p_x)$ increases in $\gamma_i \mapsto \gamma_{i+1}$. For example, in Step $(ix) \mapsto (x)$ of Figure 6.1, $-\Delta_{pot(W(p_7))} = -\Delta_{pot(p_5)} = 3 > \Delta_{pot(p_7)} = 1$. Finally, since p_{x-1} moves in $\gamma_i \mapsto \gamma_{i+1}$ (e.g., p_6 moves and makes p_7 enabled in Step $(ix) \mapsto (x)$ of Figure 6.1), we can observe that every process p_z such that $y < z < x$ (if any) moves in $\gamma_i \mapsto \gamma_{i+1}$ and is still enabled in γ_{i+1} (the first counterclockwise process starting from p_{x-2} that do not move makes its successor to be the witness of p_x) and consequently satisfies $\Delta_{pot(p_z)} = 0$ (e.g., p_6 in Step $(ix) \mapsto (x)$ of Figure 6.1). Hence, for every two process p_{y_1} and p_{y_2} such that both $pot(p_{y_1})$ and $pot(p_{y_2})$ increase, we have $W(p_{y_1}) \neq W(p_{y_2})$, i.e., Claim II below.

Claim II: *W is an injective function such that $-\Delta_{pot(W(p_x))} > \Delta_{pot(p_x)}$, for every non-root process p_x such that $\Delta_{pot(p_x)} > 0$.*

By Claims I and II, *Pot* decreases in $\gamma_i \mapsto \gamma_{i+1}$, and we are done.   □

From Remark 6.7 and Lemma 6.8, we can deduce the folloing.

Corollary 6.9   *In e, p_0 executes Action T infinitely often.*

Using Corollary 6.9 and the fact that $K \geq n$, we now show that the variable v of the root eventually takes a value that does not appear anywhere else in the ring using a *pigeonhole principle* (Lemma 6.13). From that point, the next time the root will be enabled, the configuration will be legitimate (Lemma 6.14).

Definition 6.10   Let $VNR_i = \{p_x.v : x > 0\}$ be the set of values appearing in the variable v of non-root processes in configuration γ_i. We omit the subscript when it is clear from the context.

Remark 6.11   In any configuration, we have $0 < |VNR| < n$.

For example, in the configuration depicted in Figure 6.4, $VNR = \{1, 3, 4\}$.

Lemma 6.12 $\forall t \geq 0$, *if* $\forall s \in \{0, \dots, t-1\}$, $p_0.v \in VNR_s$, *then* $VNR_t \subseteq VNR_0$.

Proof. By induction on t. First, the base case, $t = 0$, is vacuum. Assume then that $t > 0$ and $\forall s \in \{0, \dots, t-1\}$, $p_0.v \in VNR_s$. $VNR_{t-1} \subseteq VNR_0$ since either $t - 1 = 0$ and $VNR_{t-1} = VNR_0$, or $t - 1 > 0$ and $VNR_{t-1} \subseteq VNR_0$ by induction hypothesis. Moreover, every non-root process p_x that moves in $\gamma_{t-1} \mapsto \gamma_t$ sets $p_x.v$ to $\gamma_{t-1}(p_{x-1}).v$. Now, in either case (i.e., whether p_{x-1} is the root or a non-root process), $\gamma_{t-1}(p_{x-1}).v \in VNR_{t-1}$ since, by hypothesis, $p_0.v \in VNR_{t-1}$. Hence, $VNR_t \subseteq VNR_{t-1} \subseteq VNR_0$ and we are done. □

Lemma 6.13   *Let $e' = \gamma_0 \cdots \gamma_i$ be any prefix of e. If $K \geq n$ and the root p_0 has executed Action T $(n-1)$ times in e', then there exists $j \in \{0, \dots, i\}$ such that $p_0.v \notin VNR$ in γ_j.*

Proof. The root p_0 increments $p_0.v$ modulo K $(n-1)$ times in e' (see the code of Action T at p_0), with $K \geq n$. So, $p_0.v$ took exactly n different values in e'. Now, $|VNR_0| < n$ (see Remark 6.11). Thus, there exists j in $\{0, \dots, i\}$ such that $\gamma_j(p_0.v) \notin VNR_0$. Consider the minimum j subject to that condition. By Lemma 6.12, $VNR_j \subseteq VNR_0$, hence $p_0.v \notin VNR$ in γ_j. □

The lemma below claims that, once $p_0.v \notin VNR$, we have the guarantee that the configuration will be legitimate the next time p_0 is enabled.

Lemma 6.14   *Let $e' = \gamma_0 \cdots \gamma_i$ be any prefix of e. If*

- *p_0 is enabled to execute Action T in γ_i and*

- *there exists $j \in \{0, \dots, i-1\}$ such that $p_0.v \notin VNR$ in γ_j and for every $z \in \{j+1, \dots, i-1\}$, p_0 is disabled,*

then $\gamma_i \in \mathcal{L}$, i.e., γ_i is legitimate.

Proof. (The following proof is illustrated with Figure 6.1.)

In γ_j (see, for example, Configuration (v) in Figure 6.1), every non-root process p_x satisfies $p_x.v \neq p_0.v$ and so p_0 is disabled. Now, in γ_i, p_0 is enabled, i.e., $p_{n-1}.v = p_0.v$. Intuitively, since values are propagated clockwise, this implies that all variables v are equal in γ_i, i.e., the first time p_0 is enabled after γ_j (see Configuration (xii) in Figure 6.1). So, γ_i belongs to $\mathcal{L}$. We now formalize this intuition.

Claim I: $p_0.v$ *is constant all along* $\gamma_j \cdots \gamma_i$.

Proof of the claim: $p_0.v \notin VNR$ in γ_j implies that p_0 is disabled in γ_j. Moreover, by hypothesis, for every $z \in \{j+1, \dots, i-1\}$, p_0 is disabled. Hence, in the suffix of e starting from γ_j, p_0 is enabled at the earliest in γ_i and so p_0 does not move in $\gamma_j \cdots \gamma_i$.

Claim II: $\forall x \in \{1, \ldots, n-1\}$, $\exists t \in \{j+1, \ldots, i\}$ *such that* $\gamma_t(p_x).v = \gamma_i(p_0).v$.

Proof of the claim: By backward induction starting from p_{n-1}.

Since p_0 is enabled in γ_i, we have $\gamma_i(p_0).v = \gamma_i(p_0).Pred.v = \gamma_i(p_{n-1}).v$. Let $x \in \{1, \ldots, n-2\}$. First, $\gamma_j(p_{x+1}).v \neq \gamma_j(p_0).v = \gamma_i(p_0).v$ since $p_0.v \notin VNR$ in γ_j and by Claim I. Now, by induction hypothesis, $\exists t \in \{j+1, \ldots, i\}$ such that $\gamma_t(p_{x+1}).v = \gamma_i(p_0).v$. So, p_{x+1} necessarily sets $p_{x+1}.v$ to $\gamma_i(p_0).v$ in a step $\gamma_s \mapsto \gamma_{s+1}$ with $s \in \{j, \ldots, t-1\}$. So, $\gamma_s(p_x).v = \gamma_s(p_{x+1}).Pred.v = \gamma_i(p_0).v$. Finally, $s \geq j+1$ since $\gamma_j(p_x).v \neq \gamma_j(p_0).v = \gamma_i(p_0).v$, by Claim I and owing the fact that $p_0.v \notin VNR$ in γ_j.

Claim III: $\forall x \in \{0, \ldots, n-1\}$, $\forall t \in \{j, \ldots, i-1\}$, *if* $\gamma_t(p_x).v = \gamma_i(p_0).v$, *then* $\forall s \in \{t+1, \ldots, i\}$, $\gamma_s(p_x).v = \gamma_i(p_0).v$.

Proof of the claim: By contradiction. Let x be the minimum element of $\{0, \ldots, n-1\}$ satisfying $\exists t \in \{j, \ldots, i-1\}$ such that $\gamma_t(p_x).v = \gamma_i(p_0).v$ and $\exists z \in \{t+1, \ldots, i\}$ where $\gamma_z(p_x).v \neq \gamma_i(p_0).v$. First, $x \neq 0$ by Claim I. Then, $\gamma_j(p_x).v \neq \gamma_j(p_0).v = \gamma_i(p_0).v$ since $p_0.v \notin VNR$ in γ_j and by Claim I. So, $\exists w \in \{j, \ldots, t-1\}$ such that p_x sets $p_x.v$ to $\gamma_i(p_0).v$ in a step $\gamma_w \mapsto \gamma_{w+1}$ so that $\gamma_t(p_x).v = \gamma_i(p_0).v$. Now, $\gamma_w(p_x).Pred.v = \gamma_w(p_{x-1}).v = \gamma_i(p_0).v$ (see the guard of Action T for p_x). Moreover, by the minimality of x, $\forall s \in \{w, \ldots, i\}$, $\gamma_s(p_{x-1}).v = \gamma_i(p_0).v$ with $w < t$, which implies that Action T is disabled at p_x in $\gamma_t \cdots \gamma_i$, i.e., $\forall s \in \{t, \ldots, i\}$, $\gamma_s(p_x).v = \gamma_i(p_0).v$, a contradiction.

The lemma follows from Claims I–III.   □

From Lemmas 6.13 and 6.14, follows.

Corollary 6.15   *Let $e' = \gamma_0 \cdots \gamma_i$ be any prefix of e. If $K \geq n$ and p_0 is enabled to execute its nth Action T in γ_i, then $\gamma_i \in \mathcal{L}$, i.e., γ_i is legitimate.*

By Corollaries 6.9 and 6.15, we have the following.

Corollary 6.16   *If $K \geq n$, e contains a configuration of $\mathcal{L}$. (Convergence)*

By Remark 6.4, Lemma 6.5, and Corollary 6.16, Theorem 6.17 follows.

Theorem 6.17   *If $K \geq n$, then Algorithm Token is self-stabilizing for TC (i.e., the token circulation specification) in every oriented rooted ring network under the distributed unfair daemon.*

6.3.2   COMPLEXITY ANALYSIS

Memory Requirement

Since every process holds a single variable v of domain $\{0, \ldots, K-1\}$, the memory requirement of Token is in $\Theta(\log(K))$ bits per process.

We have proven that Algorithm Token is self-stabilizing under the distributed unfair daemon when $K \geq n$. Fokkink et al [FHP05] studied the question of whether or not Algorithm Token is still self-stabilizing when $K < n$. Their answer is partial: they propose a counter-example sequential execution for $K = n - 2$, and show that Algorithm Token is still self-stabilizing when $K = n - 1$ and the daemon is central unfair. Below, we show that the results of Fokkink et al. [FHP05] do not extend to the distributed unfair daemon. Indeed, for $K = n - 1$, we exhibit a synchronous execution of Algorithm Token that does not self-stabilize. In Section 6.4.2, we complete our answer by showing that there is no value $K < n - 1$ for which Algorithm Token is self-stabilizing, even if the daemon is restricted to be central strongly fair.

Let assume that $K = n - 1$ and study the synchronous execution starting from the initial configuration defined below.

1: $p_0.v = 0$
2: **for** $i = 1$ **to** $n - 1$ **do**
3:    $p_i.v = n - i - 1$
4: **end for**

In each synchronous step, all variables are incremented modulo $n - 1$. We give an illustrative example in Table 6.1 for $n = 5$. Hence, each every $n - 1$ steps, we retrieve the initial illegitimate configuration, and the next theorem follows.

Table 6.1: Fragment of non-converging execution for $K = 4 = n - 1$

$p_0 \cdot v$	$p_1 \cdot v$	$p_2 \cdot v$	$p_3 \cdot v$	$p_4 \cdot v$
0	3	2	1	0
1	0	3	2	1
2	1	0	3	2
3	2	1	0	3
0	3	2	1	0

Theorem 6.18   *If $K = n - 1$, then in every oriented rooted ring network of n processes, there exists a synchronous execution of Algorithm Token that never converges.*

We now study the overhead in memory requirement of Algorithm Token. In our model, a non self-stabilizing token ring algorithm, i.e., an algorithm that realizes the token circulation specification starting from a predefined initial configuration, can be trivially implemented using only two states per process: consider Algorithm Token with $K = 2$; starting from a configuration where all processes have their variable v equal to 0, the specification of the token circulation is satisfied. Indeed, Lemmas 6.1 and 6.5 can be still applied since their respective proof does not use K. Hence, the overhead of Token in terms of memory requirement is $\Theta(\log K)$.

However, notice that self-stabilizing solutions with a constant overhead exist, e.g., the two other solutions proposed by Dijkstra [Dij73, Dij74], respectively, use three and four states per process, yet assuming a locally central unfair daemon. Finally, Petit and Villain proposed in [PV97] a token circulation for arbitrary rooted networks assuming a distributed weakly fair daemon and using $\Theta(\log \Delta)$ bits per process, where Δ is the maximum degree of the network. Now, in a rooted ring, $\Delta = 2$.

Overhead in Time

Token circulation algorithms are often compared w.r.t. their *traversal time*, i.e., the time required by the token to make a full traversal of the network. Indeed, the main application of the token circulation is the mutual exclusion (in practice, a process performs its critical section atomically, in the statement of its action, when it releases the token). In this case, the traversal time corresponds to the *waiting time*, i.e., the maximal time for a requesting process to obtain the critical section. Now, regarding the traversal time, Algorithm Token has no overhead since starting from a legitimate configuration, the token makes a full traversal of the ring in n steps (resp. n rounds), which corresponds to the optimal complexity.

Move Complexity

We now evaluate the stabilization time of Algorithm Token in terms of moves, steps, and rounds. From Remark 6.7, Lemma 6.8, and Corollary 6.15, we can easily derive an upper bound in $O(n^3)$ on the stabilization time in steps of Algorithm Token assuming $K \geq n$ and the distributed unfair daemon. We now propose a tighter bound in $O(n^2)$ moves. To that goal, we study the *causality over the moves*. This latter technique is widely used in the self-stabilizing area, e.g., [KC99, ST07]. Basically, the heart of this technique consists in analyzing which events make a process to be enabled, either the initial configuration or some moves from its neighbors.

The reasoning below neither depends on the value of K, nor the kind of daemon. Hence, it will be reused to evaluate the step complexity of Token under a locally central daemon.

Consider now an arbitrary execution $e = \gamma_0 \cdots \gamma_i \cdots$ of Algorithm Token. Recall that e is infinite, by Lemma 6.1.

Definition 6.19   Let p_x be a process and $\gamma_i \mapsto \gamma_{i+1}$ be a step of e in which p_x moves. We identify this move by the ordered pair $M = (x, i)$. For any move M, we denote by $M.x$ (resp. $M.i$) the first element (resp. the second element) of the ordered pair M.

Definition 6.20   Let M be a move. We define the *cause* of M, noted $Cause(M)$, as follows.

- If $M.x = 0$ (i.e., M has been executed by the root p_0), then $Cause(M) = M$.

- Otherwise,

    - if $p_{M.x-1}$ (i.e., the predecessor of $p_{M.x}$) has not moved in $\gamma_0 \cdots \gamma_{M.i}$ (i.e., $\forall j \in \{0, \ldots, M.i - 1\}$, $p_{M.x-1} \notin Activated(\gamma_j, \gamma_{j+1})$), then $Cause(M) = M$,

    – otherwise, $Cause(M) = M'$, where M' is the last move executed by $p_{M.x-1}$ in $\gamma_0 \cdots \gamma_{M.i}$ (i.e., M' is the move in e satisfying $M'.x = M.x - 1$ and $M'.i < M.i$ for which $M'.i$ is maximum).

Definition 6.21   Every move M such that $Cause(M) = M$ is said to be *self-causal*. We distinguish two types of *self-causal* moves. Let M be a *self-causal* move.

- M is *root-self-causal* if $M.x = 0$.

- M is *other-self-causal* if $M.x \neq 0$.

Remark 6.22   By definition, there are at most $n - 1$ other-self-causal moves in e. Moreover, every move of the root p_0 is root-self-causal.

    In Figure 6.1, page 64, $(0, iv)$, i.e., the move of the root p_0 in $(iv) \mapsto (v)$, is a root-self-causal move. $(3, i)$ and $(7, iii)$ are other-self-causal moves. In contrast, $(4, ii)$, $(2, vi)$, and $(1, v)$ are not self-causal.

    We now consider any finite prefix $P = \gamma_0 \cdots \gamma_i$ of e.

Definition 6.23   We call *causal path* (in P) any maximal sequence of moves $M_0, \ldots, M_j$ such that for every $t \in \{1, \ldots, j\}$, $Cause(M_t) \neq M_t$ and $Cause(M_t) = M_{t-1}$. The *cost* of the causal path $M_0, \ldots, M_j$ is $j + 1$ moves. For any causal path $M_0, \ldots, M_j$, M_0 is called the *initial cause* of $M_0, \ldots, M_j$.

    Notice that, since P is assumed to be finite and $Cause(M) = M$ if $M.x = 0$, any *causal path* in P is finite. In Figure 6.1 (page 64), there are three causal paths:

- $(3, i), (4, ii), (5, v), (6, ix), (7, x)$;

- $(7, iii)$; and

- $(0, iv), (1, v), (2, vi), (3, vii), (4, viii), (5, ix), (6, x), (7, xi)$.

Remark 6.24   Let $M_0, \ldots, M_j$ be any causal path. By definition,

- since $M_0, \ldots, M_j$ is maximal, M_0 is self-causal, and

- since only M_0 is self-causal and for every $t \in \{1, \ldots, j\}$, $p_{M_{t-1}.x}$ is the predecessor of $p_{M_t.x}$, the projection of a causal path on the processes is an elementary path.

By construction, we have the following property.

Remark 6.25   Every move executed in P belongs to exactly one causal path (of P).

From the previous remark, we can deduce the following.

Corollary 6.26   *The number of moves executed in P is equal to the sum of the costs of all causal paths of P.*

In Figure 6.1 (page 64), the sum of the cost of three causal paths is 14, i.e., the number of moves in the prefix of execution given in Figure 6.1.

Remark 6.27   Let $M_0, \ldots, M_j$ be any causal path. The cost $j + 1$ of the causal path is less than or equal to $n - M_0.x$, i.e., the clockwise distance between $p_{M_0.x}$ and the root p_0 (indeed, the projection of the path on processes is elementary, see Remark 6.24).

By Remarks 6.22 and 6.25, P contains at most $n - 1$ causal paths whose initial cause is other-self-causal. Moreover, in P there are exactly X causal paths whose initial cause is root-self-causal, where X is the number of moves in P of the root p_0. Hence, in P the sum of the costs of all causal paths is less than or equal to $\frac{n(n-1)}{2} + Xn$. Hence, from Corollary 6.26, Lemma 6.28 follows.

Lemma 6.28   *In any finite prefix P of e, there are at most $\frac{n(n-1)}{2} + Xn$ moves, where X is the number of moves of the root p_0 in P.*

By Corollary 6.15, in the prefix of execution leading to the first legitimate configuration, the number of moves of the root X satisfies $X \leq n - 1$. Hence, by Lemma 6.28 and Corollary 6.9, Theorem 6.29 follows.

Theorem 6.29   *If $K \geq n$ and the daemon is distributed unfair, then the stabilization time of* Token *is at most $\frac{3n(n-1)}{2}$ moves.* (Move/Step Complexity under the Distributed Unfair Daemon.)

We now show that our bounds on the move/step complexity are tight. Indeed, below we exhibit a possible sequential execution that converges in $n(n-1) + \frac{(n-4)(n+1)}{2} + 1$ steps. This worst-case execution starts from the initial illegitimate configuration defined below.

1: $p_0.v = 0$
2: **for** $i = 1$ **to** $n - 1$ **do**
3:     $p_i.v = n - 1 - i$
4: **end for**

See the first line of Table 6.2 for an example of initial illegitimate configuration. Starting from this configuration, the execution consists in activating processes sequentially following the algorithm given below; see again Table 6.2 for an illustrative example.

```
1: for i = 1 to n − 1 do
2:     activate p₀ {p₀.v ← (p₀.v + 1) mod K}
3:     for j = n − 1 downto 1 do
4:         activate pⱼ {pⱼ.v ← pⱼ₋₁.v}
5:     end for
6: end for
7: for i = 2 to n − 3 do
8:     for j = n − 1 downto i do
9:         activate pⱼ {pⱼ.v ← pⱼ₋₁.v}
10:    end for
11: end for
12: activate pₙ₋₂
```

Actually, the execution can be split into three phases. The first phase corresponds to Lines 1–6. This phase is organized as $n - 1$ segments such that each process executes exactly one move in the segment in the following order : p_0, p_{n-1}, p_{n-2}, ..., p_1 (see Lines 2–5). At the end of the first phase, $p_0.v = n - 1$, and for every $x \in \{1, \ldots, n - 1\}$, $p_x.v = n - x$ (see Table 6.2, Line 21). The second phase, Lines 7–11, consists in repeatedly shifting the values $p_x.v$, ..., $p_{n-2}.v$ one process to the right, starting from the rightmost process p_x satisfying $p_x.v = n - 1$, by sequentially activating p_{n-1}, ..., p_{x-1}, until the system reaches a configuration containing exactly two tokens. The third phase corresponds to exactly one step (Line 12), where p_{n-2} moves, which causes the elimination of one more token and so the convergence. This execution lasts exactly $n(n - 1) + \frac{(n-4)(n+1)}{2} + 1$ steps.

Theorem 6.30   *If $K \geq n$, then there exists a sequential execution of* Token *that converges in $n(n - 1) + \frac{(n-4)(n+1)}{2} + 1$ steps.*

Round Complexity

We now show that the stabilization time of Algorithm Token assuming $K \geq n$ and an unfair daemon is at most $2n - 3$ rounds. Then, we show that this bound is reachable by a synchronous execution.

Informally, after at most $n - 1$ rounds, the root p_0 has held at least once every token that has not yet disappeared. We can show that in this execution prefix, if the system has not already reached a legitimate configuration, then it has converged to a particular subset of configurations, called *convex* configurations (see Definition 6.31 and Lemma 6.36). In this latter case, the system reaches, within at most $n - 2$ additional rounds, a legitimate configuration (see Lemma 6.35). Hence, we obtain an upper bound of $2n - 3$ rounds (see Theorem 6.37). Below, we formalize this sketch of proof.

Table 6.2: Worst-case execution for $K \geq n = 5$

	$p_0 \cdot v$	$p_1 \cdot v$	$p_2 \cdot v$	$p_3 \cdot v$	$p_4 \cdot v$
1:	0	3	2	1	0
Phase I					
2:	1	3	2	1	0
3:	1	3	2	1	1
4:	1	3	2	2	1
5:	1	3	3	2	1
6:	1	1	3	2	1
7:	2	1	3	2	1
8:	2	1	3	2	2
9:	2	1	3	3	2
10:	2	1	1	3	2
11:	2	2	1	3	2
12:	3	2	1	3	2
13:	3	2	1	3	3
14:	3	2	1	1	3
15:	3	2	2	1	3
16:	3	3	2	1	3
17:	4	3	2	1	3
18:	4	3	2	1	1
19:	4	3	2	2	1
20:	4	3	3	2	1
21:	4	4	3	2	1
Phase II					
22:	4	4	3	2	2
23:	4	4	3	3	2
24:	4	4	4	3	2
Phase III					
25:	4	4	4	4	2

Let $e = \gamma_0 \cdots \gamma_i \cdots$ be an execution of Algorithm Token.

Definition 6.31   A configuration γ_i is *convex* if $\exists x \in \{0, \ldots, n-1\}$ such that $\forall y \in \{0, \ldots, x\}$, $p_y.v = p_0.v$ and $\forall z \in \{x+1, \ldots, n-1\}$, $p_z.v \neq p_0.v$. The *weight* of a convex configuration γ_i, noted $w(\gamma_i)$, is the maximum index $x \in \{0, \ldots, n-1\}$ such that $p_x.v = p_0.v$.

Remark 6.32   For every convex configuration γ_i, we have:

- $0 \leq w(\gamma_i) \leq n-1$,

- if $w(\gamma_i) \in \{n-2, n-1\}$, then $\gamma_i \in \mathcal{L}$, and

- $\forall x, 1 \leq x \leq w(\gamma_i)$, p_x is disabled in γ_i.

Lemma 6.33   *Let γ_i be a convex configuration. If p_0 is enabled, then $\gamma_i \in \mathcal{L}$.*

Proof. By definition of Action T at p_0, $p_0.v = p_{n-1}.v$ in γ_i. So, $w(\gamma_i) = n-1$ and we are done by Remark 6.32. $\qquad\square$

Lemma 6.34   *Let $\gamma_i \mapsto \gamma_{i+1}$ a step of e such that γ_i is convex and p_0 does not move in $\gamma_i \mapsto \gamma_{i+1}$. Then, γ_{i+1} is convex and $w(\gamma_{i+1}) \geq w(\gamma_i)$.*

Proof. First $w(\gamma_i) < n-1$, because otherwise only p_0 is enabled in γ_i. Then, since p_0 does not move in $\gamma_i \mapsto \gamma_{i+1}$, $\gamma_i(p_0).v = \gamma_{i+1}(p_0).v$.

Assume now, by contradiction, γ_{i+1} is not convex. By definition, this means that there exists $x \in \{1, \ldots, n-1\}$ such that $p_x.v = p_0.v$ and $p_{x-1}.v \neq p_0.v$ in γ_{i+1}.

- If $\gamma_i(p_{x-1}).v = \gamma_i(p_0).v$, then $\gamma_{i+1}(p_{x-1}).v = \gamma_i(p_0).v$ since either $x-1 = 0$ and, by hypothesis, p_0 does not move in $\gamma_i \mapsto \gamma_{i+1}$; or $x-1 > 0$ and, as by hypothesis γ_i is convex, p_{x-1} is disabled in γ_i (see Remark 6.32). Now, we already know that $\gamma_i(p_0).v = \gamma_{i+1}(p_0).v$. Hence, we can conclude that $\gamma_{i+1}(p_{x-1}).v = \gamma_{i+1}(p_0).v$, a contradiction.

- Otherwise, $\gamma_i(p_{x-1}).v \neq \gamma_i(p_0).v$. Since γ_i is convex, $\gamma_i(p_x).v \neq \gamma_i(p_0).v$ too. Then, whether or not p_x moves, $\gamma_{i+1}(p_x).v \in \{\gamma_i(p_x).v, \gamma_i(p_{x-1}).v\}$. Hence, $\gamma_{i+1}(p_x).v \neq \gamma_i(p_0).v = \gamma_{i+1}(p_0).v$, a contradiction.

Hence, γ_{i+1} is convex. Assume now, by contradiction, that $w(\gamma_{i+1}) < w(\gamma_i)$. Let $x = w(\gamma_i)$. Since γ_{i+1} is convex, we necessarily have $\gamma_{i+1}(p_x).v \neq \gamma_{i+1}(p_0).v = \gamma_i(p_0).v$. Now, by definition, $\gamma_i(p_x).v = \gamma_i(p_0).v$ and p_x does not move in $\gamma_i \mapsto \gamma_{i+1}$ because either $x = 0$ and, by hypothesis, p_0 does not move in $\gamma_i \mapsto \gamma_{i+1}$; or $x > 0$ and, as by hypothesis γ_i is convex, p_x is disabled (see Remark 6.32). Hence, $\gamma_{i+1}(p_x).v = \gamma_i(p_0).v = \gamma_{i+1}(p_0).v$ and so $w(\gamma_{i+1}) \geq w(\gamma_i)$, a contradiction. $\qquad\square$

Lemma 6.35   *Let $Pref = \gamma_0 \cdots \gamma_i$ be a prefix of e such that γ_0 is convex. If $Pref$ lasts exactly $n - 2$ rounds, then $Pref$ contains a legitimate configuration.*

Proof. First, if p_0 moves during $Pref$, we are done by Lemmas 6.33 and 6.34.

Assume now that p_0 does not move in $Pref$. Then, $p_0.v$ is constant all along $Pref$. Let α be the value of $p_0.v$ in $Pref$. If there is a configuration γ_j in $Pref$ such that $w(\gamma_j) \in \{n - 2, n - 1\}$ we are done by Remark 6.32 and Lemma 6.34. Assume now that $w(\gamma_j) < n - 2$ in all configurations γ_j of $Pref$. Then, by Remark 6.32, $0 \leq w(\gamma_j) < n - 2$. It is then sufficient to show that the weight of the configurations increases at each round. Let $\gamma_{R_0} = \gamma_0$ and, for every $s > 0$, let γ_{R_s} be the last configuration of the sth round. (So, $\gamma_{R_{n-2}} = \gamma_i$, the last configuration of $Pref$.)

Claim I: *for every $j \in \{0, \ldots, n - 3\}$, we have $w(\gamma_{R_j}) < w(\gamma_{R_{j+1}})$.*

Proof of the claim: By Lemma 6.34, $p_{w(\gamma_{R_j})}.v = \alpha$ all along $\gamma_{R_j} \cdots \gamma_{R_{j+1}}$. But, $p_{w(\gamma_{R_j})+1}.v \neq \alpha$ in γ_{R_j}. So, $p_{w(\gamma_{R_j})+1}$ necessarily sets $p_{w(\gamma_{R_j})+1}.v$ to α in $\gamma_{R_j} \cdots \gamma_{R_{j+1}}$, and by Lemma 6.34, we are done.

The lemma follows from Claim I.   □

Lemma 6.36   *Let $Pref = \gamma_0 \cdots \gamma_i$ be any prefix of e. If $Pref$ lasts exactly $n - 1$ rounds, then $Pref$ contains a configuration γ_j such that $\gamma_j \in \mathcal{L}$ or γ_j is convex.*

Proof. Let $\sharp T$ be the number of times the root p_0 executes Action T in $Pref$. We consider the following three cases.

1. $\sharp T = 0$. Then, all along $Pref$, $p_0.v$ is constant. Let α be the value of $p_0.v$ in $Pref$. We now show, by induction, that after $x \leq n - 2$ rounds from γ_0, $\forall y \in \{0, \ldots, x\}$, $p_y.v = \alpha$ until (at least) the end of $Pref$. The base case ($x = 0$) is trivial. Let $0 < x \leq n - 2$. After, $x - 1$ rounds from γ_0, $\forall y \in \{0, \ldots, x - 1\}$, $p_y.v = \alpha$ until (at least) the end of $Pref$, by induction hypothesis. If $p_x.v = \alpha$, then p_x is disabled until (at least) the end of $Pref$. Otherwise, $p_x.v \neq \alpha$ at the beginning of the xth round. Now, since $x > 0$, along the xth round, p_x satisfies $Token(p_x)$ while $p_x.v \neq \alpha$, so p_x executes Action T during the xth round and we retrieve the previous case. Thus, the induction holds: after x rounds from γ_0, $\forall y \in \{0, \ldots, x\}$, $p_y.v = \alpha$ until the end of $Pref$.

   We now apply the previous result with $x = n - 2$. Then, in the last configuration of the $(n - 2)^{th}$ round, all processes, except maybe p_{n-1}, have the same value α in their variable v: the configuration is legitimate.

2. $0 < \sharp T < n - 1$. Then, $p_0.v$ took $\sharp T + 1$ distinct values in $Pref$ since $T + 1 < n$. Let α be the value of $p_0.v$ after the last incrementation in $Pref$. $p_0.v$ successively took values $\alpha - \sharp T, \ldots, \alpha - 1, \alpha$ in $Pref$ and $p_0.v = \alpha$ in the last configuration of $Pref$.

We reuse the notation γ_{R_s} (for every $s > 0$), introduced in Lemma 6.35. We show, by induction on j, that $\forall x \in \{0, \ldots, j\}$:

(a) $p_x.v \in \{\alpha - \sharp T, \ldots, \alpha - 1, \alpha\}$ in all configurations of $\gamma_{R_j} \cdots \gamma_{R_{n-1}}$ (i.e., from the end of the jth round to the end of *Pref*);

(b) if $p_x.v = \alpha$ in some configuration γ_t in $\gamma_{R_j} \cdots \gamma_{R_{n-1}}$, then $\forall s \in \{t, \ldots, R_{n-1}\}, \forall y \in \{0, \ldots, x\}, p_y.v = \alpha$ in γ_s.

For $j = 0$, the induction trivially holds since $p_0.v \in \{\alpha - \sharp T, \ldots, \alpha - 1, \alpha\}$ all along *Pref* and α is the last value taken by $p_0.v$ in *Pref*.

Assume now that $j > 0$.

(a) In $\gamma_{R_{j-1}} \cdots \gamma_{R_{n-1}}$, $\forall x \in \{0, \ldots, j - 1\}$, $p_x.v \in \{\alpha - \sharp T, \ldots, \alpha - 1, \alpha\}$, by induction hypothesis. Notice that this is in particular true for p_{j-1}. So, $p_{j-1}.v \in \{\alpha - \sharp T, \ldots, \alpha - 1, \alpha\}$ continuously during $\gamma_{R_{j-1}} \cdots \gamma_{R_j}$, which lasts exactly one round. Consequently, $p_j.v \in \{\alpha - \sharp T, \ldots, \alpha - 1, \alpha\}$ in some configuration of $\gamma_{R_{j-1}} \cdots \gamma_{R_j}$ (if $p_j.v \notin \{\alpha - \sharp T, \ldots, \alpha - 1, \alpha\}$ in $\gamma_{R_{j-1}}$, then p_j necessarily executes Action T to set $p_j.v$ to some value in $\{\alpha - \sharp T, \ldots, \alpha - 1, \alpha\}$ during $\gamma_{R_{j-1}} \cdots \gamma_{R_j}$). So, $p_j.v \in \{\alpha - \sharp T, \ldots, \alpha - 1, \alpha\}$ in some configuration of $\gamma_{R_{j-1}} \cdots \gamma_{R_j}$. In this case, we are done because, from that point, $p_j.v$ cannot be switched to any value outside $\{\alpha - \sharp T, \ldots, \alpha - 1, \alpha\}$ until the end of *Pref* because of p_{j-1}.

(b) Finally, assume that $p_j.v = \alpha$ in some configuration γ_t in $\gamma_{R_j} \cdots \gamma_{R_{n-1}}$. Consider the following two subcases.

  • There exists $s \in \{R_{j-1}, \ldots, t - 1\}$, such that $p_j.v$ is set to α in $\gamma_s \mapsto \gamma_{s+1}$ by executing Action T. In this case, $\gamma_s(p_j).Pred.v = \gamma_s(p_{j-1}).v = \alpha$ (*Token*(p_j) holds in γ_s for $j > 0$) and by induction hypothesis, $\forall y \in \{0, \ldots, j - 1\}, p_y.v = \alpha$ all along $\gamma_s \cdots \gamma_{R_{n-1}}$. Notice that, this is in particular true for p_{j-1}. So, $p_j.v = \alpha$ from γ_{s+1} to the end of *Pref*. Since $s + 1 \leq t$, we are done.

  • For every $s \in \{R_{j-1}, \ldots, t\}$, $p_j.v = \alpha$ in γ_s. As $t \geq R_j$, $\gamma_{R_{j-1}} \cdots \gamma_t$ contains at least one round. Since $j > 0$, there is at least one configuration γ_w in $\gamma_{R_{j-1}} \cdots \gamma_t$ where $\neg Token(p_j) \equiv p_{j-1}.v = p_j.v = \alpha$ holds (otherwise p_j necessarily executes action T in $\gamma_{R_{j-1}} \cdots \gamma_t$ to modify $p_j.v$). By induction hypothesis, from γ_w to the end of *Pref*, $\forall y \in \{0, \ldots, j - 1\}, p_y.v = \alpha$ (this is in particular true for p_{j-1}), and so $p_j.v$ is. As $w \leq t$, we are done.

Since $\gamma_{R_{n-1}} = \gamma_i$ and $p_0.v = \alpha$, we can deduce from the previous induction that γ_i is convex.

3. $\sharp T \geq n - 1$. In this case, there exists a configuration $\gamma_j \in Pref$ where $p_0.v \notin VNR$ (Lemma 6.13, page 70). By definition, γ_j is convex, and we are done.

□

From Lemmas 6.35 and 6.36, Theorem 6.37 follows.

Theorem 6.37   *If* $K \geq n$ *and the daemon is distributed unfair, then the stabilization time of* Token *is at most* $2n - 3$ *rounds.* (Round Complexity under the Distributed Unfair Daemon.)

We now show that the upper bound given in the previous theorem is reachable. To that goal, consider an synchronous execution starting from the initial illegitimate configuration defined below.

1: $p_0.v = 0$
2: **for** $i = 1$ **to** $n - 1$ **do**
3:    $p_i.v = n - 1 - i$
4: **end for**

An example execution for $n = 5$ is given in Table 6.3. The synchronous execution contains 7 steps, i.e., $7 = 2 \times 5 - 3 = 2 \times n - 3$ rounds (recall that in synchronous settings, one step exactly corresponds to one round).

Table 6.3: Worst-case execution for $K \geq n = 5$

	$p_0 \cdot v$	$p_1 \cdot v$	$p_2 \cdot v$	$p_3 \cdot v$	$p_4 \cdot v$
1:	0	3	2	1	0
2:	1	0	3	2	1
3:	2	1	0	3	2
4:	3	2	1	0	3
5:	4	3	2	1	0
6:	4	4	3	2	1
7:	4	4	4	3	2
8:	4	4	4	4	3

In the initial illegitimate configuration, all processes are enabled. Then, in each of the $n - 1$ first steps, all processes move. In particular, p_0 increments $n - 1$ times. Hence, after $n - 1$ steps (e.g., 4 steps to reach Configuration 5 in Table 6.3), the configuration becomes convex in accordance to Case 3 in the proof of Lemma 6.36. Then, according to Lemma 6.35, $n - 2$ steps are necessary so that the value of p_0 propagates to p_{n-2} (i.e., 3 steps to reach Configuration 8 in Table 6.3). After that, the configuration is legitimate.

Theorem 6.38   *If* $K \geq n$, *then there exists a sequential execution of* Token *that converges in* $2n - 3$ *rounds.*

6.4 STUDY ASSUMING $K \geq n - 1$ AND A LOCALLY CENTRAL UNFAIR DAEMON

Several results proven in Section 6.3 actually neither depend on the value of K, nor the kind of daemon. So, we will reuse some of these results in this section.

6.4.1 PROOF OF SELF-STABILIZATION

The proof for $K \geq n$ and the distributed unfair daemon can be easily adapted to work assuming $K \geq n - 1$ under a local central unfair daemon replacing Lemma 6.13 by Lemma 6.40, this latter uses the technical result given in Lemma 6.39 below.

Lemma 6.39   *Let $e' = \gamma_0 \cdots \gamma_i$ be any prefix of e. If*

- *the root p_0 executes Action T for the first time in $\gamma_{j-1} \mapsto \gamma_j$ (with $1 \leq j \leq i - 1$), and*

- *the root p_0 executes Action T for the second time in $\gamma_{i-1} \mapsto \gamma_i$,*

then there exists $w \in \{j + 1, \ldots, i - 1\}$ such that $|VNR| < n - 1$ in γ_w.

Proof. Let $\gamma_j(p_o).v = \alpha$. Then, as p_0 executes Action T in $\gamma_{j-1} \mapsto \gamma_j$, we have $\gamma_{j-1}(p_0).v = \alpha - 1 = \gamma_{j-1}(p_0).Pred.v = \gamma_{j-1}(p_{n-1}).v$ (see Algorithm 6.5). By definition of the locally central daemon, $\gamma_j(p_{n-1}).v = \gamma_{j-1}(p_{n-1}).v = \alpha - 1$. Moreover, we have $\gamma_{i-1}(p_0).v = \gamma_{i-1}(p_0).Pred.v = \gamma_{i-1}(p_{n-1}).v = \alpha$ since p_0 is enabled in γ_{i-1} to set $p_0.v$ to $\alpha + 1$ by Action T. Hence, there exists $w \in \{j + 1, \ldots, i - 1\}$ such that p_{n-1} executes $p_{n-1}.v \leftarrow \alpha$ by Action T in $\gamma_{w-1} \mapsto \gamma_w$. Thus, $\gamma_{w-1}(p_{n-2}).v = \gamma_{w-1}(p_{n-1}).Pred.v = \alpha$, and by definition of the locally central daemon, $\gamma_w(p_{n-2}).v = \alpha$ too. Hence, $\gamma_w(p_{n-2}).v = \alpha = \gamma_w(p_{n-1}).v$, i.e., $|VNR_w| < n - 1$ with $w \in \{j + 1, \ldots, i - 1\}$. $\square$

   In the proof of the next lemma, we can use Lemma 6.12, since it has been established independently of the value of K and the kind of daemon.

Lemma 6.40   *Let $e' = \gamma_0 \cdots \gamma_i$ be any prefix of e. If $K \geq n - 1$ and the root p_0 has executed Action T $(n - 1)$ times in e', then there exists $j \in \{0, \ldots, i\}$ such that $p_0.v \notin VNR$ in γ_j.*

Proof. Let $1 \leq x < y < i$ such that p_0 executes T for the first time in $\gamma_{x-1} \mapsto \gamma_x$ and for the second time in $\gamma_{y-1} \mapsto \gamma_y$ (n.b., x and y are well defined since $n \geq 3$). By Lemma 6.39, there exists $w \in \{x + 1, \ldots, y - 1\}$ such that $|VNR| < n - 1$ in γ_w. Now, between γ_w and γ_i, p_0 has incremented $p_0.v$ modulo K exactly $n - 2$ times since $x < w < y$. So, in $\gamma_w \cdots \gamma_i$, $p_0.v$ took exactly $n - 1$ different values. Thus, there exists j in $\{w, \ldots, i\}$ such that $\gamma_j(p_0.v) \notin VNR_w$. Consider the minimum j subject to that condition. By Lemma 6.12, $VNR_j \subseteq VNR_w$, hence $p_0.v \notin VNR$ in γ_j. $\square$

Then, Lemma 6.40 together with Lemma 6.14 (whose proof is independent of the value of K and the kind of daemon) gives the following corollary.

Corollary 6.41   *Let $e' = \gamma_0 \cdots \gamma_i$ be any prefix of e. If $K \geq n - 1$ and p_0 is enabled to execute its nth Action T in γ_i, then $\gamma_i \in \mathcal{L}$, i.e., γ_i is legitimate.*

By Corollaries 6.9 and 6.41, we have the guarantee that Algorithm Token still converges if $K = n - 1$ assuming a locally central unfair daemon. Hence, Theorem 6.42 follows.

Theorem 6.42   *If $K \geq n - 1$, then Algorithm Token is self-stabilizing for TC (i.e., the token circulation specification) in every oriented rooted ring network under the locally central daemon.*

6.4.2   COMPLEXITY ANALYSIS

Memory Requirement

Even assuming a locally central unfair daemon, Token is in $\Omega(\log(n))$ bits per process since $K \geq n - 1$. Below, we show the memory requirement of Token cannot be enhanced: for every $K \leq n - 2$, there is a central strongly fair execution of Token that does not converge.

First, if $K < 2$, then processes have 0 or 1 state. In this case, the token circulation has trivially no solution. Hence, without loss of generality, assume $2 \leq K \leq n - 2$. We consider the initial illegitimate configuration defined below.

```
1: p₀.v = 0
2: for i = 1 to K do
3:    pᵢ.v = K − i
4: end for
5: for i = K + 1 to n − 1 do
6:    pᵢ.v = 0
7: end for
```

An example of this initial illegitimate configuration for $K = 5$ and $n = 8$ is given in Figure 6.6. Starting from this configuration, the execution consists in activating processes sequentially following the algorithm given below.

```
1: while true do
2:    for j = 1 to K do
3:       for i = K to 1 {Step −1} do
4:          activate pᵢ {pᵢ.v ← pᵢ₋₁.v}
5:       end for
6:       activate p₀ {p₀.v ← (p₀.v + 1) mod K}
7:       for i = K + 1 to n − 1 do
8:          activate pᵢ {pᵢ.v ← pᵢ₋₁.v}
9:       end for
```

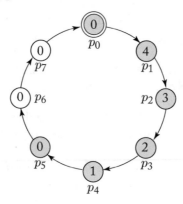

Figure 6.6: Example of initial configuration with $K = 5$.

10:    **end for**
11: **end while**

Actually, the execution is built as an infinite sequence of segments. Each segment consists of n steps and is executed following Lines 3–9. During a segment, each process is activated exactly once. Hence the execution is sequential and strongly fair.

In the final configuration γ_n of a segment $\gamma_0 \cdots \gamma_n$, every process p_x satisfies $\gamma_n(p_x).v = (\gamma_0(p_x).v + 1) \mod K$, i.e., during a segment, each process increments its variable once modulo K. Hence, after every K segments, we retrieve the initial configuration: the infinite execution never converges.

A segment is executed as follows: processes p_K, ..., p_1 sequentially moves to copy the value of their predecessor (Lines 3–5); see Configurations $(i) - (vii)$ in Figure 6.7. Then, p_0 increments its value modulo K (Line 6); see Step $(vii) \mapsto (viii)$ in Figure 6.7. Finally, processes p_{K+1}, ..., p_{n-1} sequentially move to copy the value of their predecessor (Lines 7–9); see Configurations $(viii) - (ix)$ in Figure 6.7. As expected, in Configuration (ix), every process has incremented its variable by one modulo K compared to (i).

Theorem 6.43   *If $K < n - 1$, then in every oriented rooted ring network of n processes, there exists an execution under the central strongly fair daemon of Algorithm* Token *that never converges.*

Time Complexity
We first consider the move/step complexity. Since Lemma 6.28 (page 75) and Corollaries 6.9 (page 69) of Section 6.3 have been established independently of the value of K and the kind of daemon, we can deduce the theorem below, by Lemma 6.28 and Corollaries 6.9 and 6.41. The

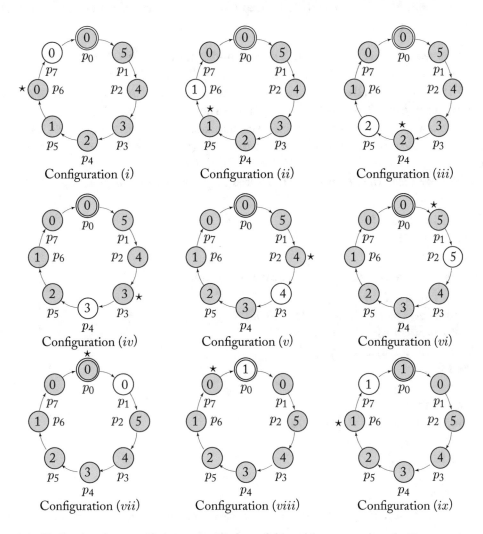

Figure 6.7: Example of non-stabilizing execution of Algorithm Token, with $K = n - 2 = 6$.

move complexity bound we obtain is then identical to the one obtained in case of a distributed unfair daemon with $K \geq n$ (Theorem 6.29, page 75).

Theorem 6.44   *If $K \geq n - 1$ and the daemon is locally central unfair, then the stabilization time of* Token *is at most $\frac{3n(n-1)}{2}$ moves.* (Move/Step Complexity under the Locally Central Unfair Daemon.)

We now show that the previous upper bound is tight. Indeed, below we exhibit a possible sequential execution that converges in $n(n-2) + \frac{(n-4)(n+1)}{2} + 1$ when $K = n - 1$ (Theorem 6.45). Recall that for all other values we have already exhibited possible sequential executions that converges in $n(n-1) + \frac{(n-4)(n+1)}{2} + 1$ steps (Theorem 6.30, page 76).

The worst-case sequential execution is very similar to the case $K \geq n$. Indeed, it starts from the same initial illegitimate configuration and the strategy followed by the daemon is almost the same.

Below we recall the definition of the initial illegitimate configuration.

1: $p_0.v = 0$
2: **for** $i = 1$ **to** $n - 1$ **do**
3:    $p_i.v = n - 1 - i$
4: **end for**

Then, the strategy is given by the algorithm below.

1: **for** $i = 1$ **to** $n - 2$ **do**
2:    activate p_0 $\{p_0.v \leftarrow (p_0.v + 1) \bmod K\}$
3:    **for** $j = n - 1$ **to** 1 {Step -1} **do**
4:       activate p_j $\{p_j.v \leftarrow p_{j-1}.v\}$
5:    **end for**
6: **end for**
7: **for** $i = 2$ **to** $n - 3$ **do**
8:    **for** $j = n - 1$ **to** i {Step -1} **do**
9:       activate p_j $\{p_j.v \leftarrow p_{j-1}.v\}$
10:    **end for**
11: **end for**
12: activate p_{n-2}

The first phase (Lines 1–6) is identical to Phase I of case $K \geq n$, except that it contains one less segment. Phases II and III (Lines 7–12) are syntactically the same as Phases II and III of case $K \geq n$. Hence, the execution is n steps shorter than the sequential execution when $K \geq n$: it lasts $n(n-2) + \frac{(n-4)(n+1)}{2} + 1$ steps. An illustrative example is given in Table 6.4.

Table 6.4: Worst-case execution for $K \geq n - 1 = 4$

	$p_0 \cdot v$	$p_1 \cdot v$	$p_2 \cdot v$	$p_3 \cdot v$	$p_4 \cdot v$
1:	0	3	2	1	0
Phase I					
2:	1	3	2	1	0
3:	1	3	2	1	1
4:	1	3	2	2	1
5:	1	3	3	2	1
6:	1	1	3	2	1
7:	2	1	3	2	1
8:	2	1	3	2	2
9:	2	1	3	3	2
10:	2	1	1	3	2
11:	2	2	1	3	2
12:	3	2	1	3	2
13:	3	2	1	3	3
14:	3	2	1	1	3
15:	3	2	2	1	3
16:	3	3	2	1	3
Phase II					
17:	3	3	2	1	1
18:	3	3	2	2	1
19:	3	3	3	2	1
Phase III					
20:	3	3	3	3	1

Theorem 6.45   *If $K = n - 1$, then there exists a sequential execution of* Token *that converges in* $n(n - 2) + \frac{(n-4)(n+1)}{2} + 1$ *steps.*

We now study the round complexity. By definition, the upper bound obtained for $K \geq n$ assuming a distributed unfair daemon still holds assuming a locally central unfair daemon. So we consider the only remaining case, i.e., $K = n - 1$. We obtain a bound larger than the one proven in the case $K \geq n$, but still in $O(n)$ rounds.

Theorem 6.46   *If $K = n - 1$ and the daemon is locally central unfair, then the stabilization time of* Token *is at most $3(n - 2) + 1$ rounds.* (Round Complexity under the Locally Central Unfair Daemon.)

Proof. The proof follows the same scheme as the one of Lemma 6.36 (page 79): let $Pref = \gamma_0 \cdots \gamma_i$ be any prefix of execution that last $n - 1$ rounds. Let $\sharp T$ be the number of times the root p_0 executes Action T in $Pref$. We consider the following four cases.

1. $\sharp T = 0$. In this case, the reasoning is identical to Case 1 in the proof of Lemma 6.36. We can then conclude that within at most $n - 2$ rounds from γ_0, the system reaches a legitimate configuration.

2. $0 < \sharp T < n - 2$. By a reasoning similar to Case 2 in the proof of Lemma 6.36, we can conclude that the last configuration γ_i of $Pref$ is convex, and by Lemma 6.35 (page 79), within at most $n - 2$ additional rounds from γ_i the configuration is legitimate. Overall, the system converges in at most $2(n - 2) + 1$ rounds in this case.

3. $\sharp T = n - 2$. Consider the next period P of $n - 2$ rounds starting from γ_i, the last configuration of $Pref$. If p_0 executes no Action T in P, then we can conclude the system reaches a legitimate configuration during that time using a reasoning which is identical to Case 1. Otherwise, p_0 executes Action T at least once in P, i.e., at least $n - 1$ times in the prefix made of $Pref$ followed by P, and using a reasoning similar to Case 2 in the proof of Lemma 6.36 (just replace Lemma 6.13 by Lemma 6.40, page 82), we can deduce that $Pref$ contains a convex configuration γ_j. Within at most $n - 2$ rounds from γ_j, the configuration is legitimate, by Lemma 6.35, page 79. Overall, the system converges in at most $3(n - 2) + 1$ rounds in this case.

4. $\sharp T \geq n - 1$. Using the same reasoning as in Case 3 in the proof of Lemma 6.36 (just replace Lemma 6.13 by Lemma 6.40, page 82), we can deduce that $Pref$ contains a convex configuration γ_j, and, by Lemma 6.35 (page 79), within at most $n - 2$ additional rounds from γ_j the configuration is legitimate. Overall, the system stabilizes in at most $2(n - 2) + 1$ rounds.

$\square$

We conjecture that the previous upper bound can be further refined. However, notice that this latter bound can be asymptotically reached. Indeed, the worst-case sequential execution proposed for Theorem 6.45 (page 87) lasts $\Omega(n)$ rounds (precisely, $2n - 5$ rounds).

CHAPTER 7

Hierarchical Collateral Composition

The reuse of algorithms is a major concern in computer science. In self-stabilization, this reuse is implemented *via* the notion of *composition*. Another important purpose of composition is to simplify both the design and the proofs of self-stabilizing algorithms.

A composition is usually modeled using a binary operator, say ∘, over two distributed algorithms A and B, called *sub-algorithms* in the sequel. This operator defines how the two sub-algorithms run together. The resulting algorithm, noted B ∘ A, is called a *composite algorithm*.

Notice that a composite algorithm is meant to be an algorithm defined in the considered model. So, the composition operator should be carefully formalized as it should not increase the expressive power of the model. That is, it should not assume properties that cannot be implemented in the model. In other words, there must exist a rewriting method to translate the composite algorithm into an algorithm that achieves the same specification, yet without using the composition operator.

Composition is a popular way to design self-stabilizing algorithms [Tel01]. Indeed, various composition techniques have been introduced, e.g., *collateral composition* [GH91, Her92b], *fair composition* [Dol00], *cross-over composition* [BGJ01], and *conditional composition* [DGPV01]; and many self-stabilizing algorithms are actually composite algorithms, e.g., [KC99, BFP14, FYHY14, DDH+16, ADD17].

Each of those aforementioned composition techniques allows to implement one of the two following algorithmic design patterns.

1. The former approach involves first the design of a self-stabilizing algorithm that emulates the behavior of a strong daemon assuming a weaker one, e.g., a self-stabilizing token circulation can be used to emulate a central daemon under a distributed daemon assumption. Then, one can design a self-stabilizing algorithm for a desired specification assuming a central daemon.

   The composition then makes the first algorithm controlling the execution of the second one so that it respects the specification of the strong daemon. Consequently, the composite algorithm self-stabilizes to the expected specification under the more general daemon (in our example, a distributed daemon).

To enforce sequentiality in our example, the composition enables a process to execute an action of the second algorithm right before releasing the token only.

2. The latter approach consists of first self-stabilizingly solving the desired specification on a restricted class of networks, say $\mathcal{N}'$ (e.g., trees or rings), and then bringing the solution to a more general class of topologies, say $\mathcal{N}$ with $\mathcal{N}' \subsetneq \mathcal{N}$ (usually arbitrary connected networks).

To that goal, we implement a self-stabilizing algorithm that builds a virtual structure of type $\mathcal{N}'$ (e.g., a spanning tree) on the top of a network of type $\mathcal{N}$. Then, in the composition, the algorithm for topologies $\mathcal{N}'$ runs on a network of type $\mathcal{N}$, but only considering the links belonging to the virtual structure, which is eventually of type $\mathcal{N}'$.

The first approach can be applied using the *cross-over composition* [BGJ01], for example. In this chapter, we focus on the *hierarchical collateral composition* introduced in [DLD$^+$13]. This composition technique allows to apply the second approach, and is actually a straightforward variant of the *collateral composition* introduced by Herman [Her92b]. In the collateral composition, the composition of two algorithms just consists of running the two algorithms concurrently. The second algorithm usually takes the output of the first one as input. For example, the first algorithm can be a silent spanning tree construction and the second one can be an algorithm dedicated for tree topologies that takes the output parent pointers of the first one as input. Hence, once the first algorithm has converged, the second one is in an arbitrary configuration, except that the parent pointers are constant and describe a spanning tree. From that point, the stabilizing property of the second algorithm ensures the overall stabilization of the composite algorithm.

The hierarchical variant of the collateral composition is justified by the following problem. When two actions are enabled at the same process but in two different algorithms of the composition, the process *nondeterministically* executes one or the other, if activated by the daemon. The hierarchical collateral composition solves this nondeterminism using local priorities: in the hierarchical collateral composition of A and B, the code of the local algorithm B(p) (for every process p) is modified so that p executes an enabled action of B(p) only when it has no enabled action in A(p). Thus, locally at each process, actions of A have priority over actions of B. However, we should underline that the priorities are only local: an enabled action of B can be executed by some process p (in particular because p has no enabled action in A), while other processes in the network have enabled actions in A.

In the next section we formally define the hierarchical collateral composition and establish a sufficient condition to show the silent self-stabilization of a composite algorithm under the distributed weakly fair daemon. In Section 7.2, we apply the composition to a simple case study. In Section 7.3, we further justify the use of local priorities.

7.1 HIERARCHICAL COLLATERAL COMPOSITION

7.1.1 DEFINITION

Recall that the hierarchical collateral composition aims at solving the nondeterminism of the collateral composition as follows: when we compose two distributed algorithms A and B, we modify the code of the local algorithm $B(p)$, for every process p, so that p executes an action of $B(p)$ only when it has no enabled action in $A(p)$. Hence, hierarchical collateral composition is defined as follows.

Definition 7.1 Hierarchical Collateral Composition. Let A and B be two distributed algorithms. The *hierarchical collateral composition* of A and B is the distributed algorithm $B \circ A$, where the local algorithm of every process p, noted $(B \circ A)(p)$, is defined as follows.

- $(B \circ A)(p)$ contains all variables of $A(p)$ and $B(p)$ (some variables may be common to $A(p)$ and $B(p)$, e.g., some outputs of $A(p)$ may be inputs in $B(p)$).

- $(B \circ A)(p)$ contains all actions of $A(p)$.

- Every action $L_i :: G_i \rightarrow S_i$ of $B(p)$ is rewritten in $(B \circ A)(p)$ as the action

$$L_i :: \neg C_p \wedge G_i \rightarrow S_i,$$

where C_p is the disjunction of all guards of all actions in $A(p)$.

By convention, $\circ$ is *right-associative*.

7.1.2 A SUFFICIENT CONDITION

Below, we present several properties of the *hierarchical collateral composition* related to both correctness and round complexity: Lemmas 7.5–7.8 and Theorem 7.12. Theorem 7.12 states a sufficient condition to show the silent self-stabilization of a composite algorithm under a distributed weakly fair daemon. To prove these properties, we first need to define the notions of *minimal relevant subsequence* and *projection*.

Definition 7.2 MRS. Let s be a sequence of configurations. The *minimal relevant subsequence* of s, noted $\mathcal{MRS}(s)$, is the maximal subsequence of s where no two consecutive configurations are identical.

Let $s = \gamma_0 \cdots \gamma_i \cdots$ and $\mathcal{MRS}(s) = \alpha_0 \cdots \alpha_j \cdots$ For every $j \geq 0$, we denote by $\gamma_{\xi(j)}$ the first configuration in s that *provides* the jth value α_j in $\mathcal{MRS}(s)$, i.e., the configuration $\gamma_{\xi(j)}$ of s which satisfies $\mathcal{MRS}(\gamma_0 \cdots \gamma_{\xi(j)}) = \alpha_0 \cdots \alpha_j$, but $\mathcal{MRS}(\gamma_0 \cdots \gamma_{\xi(j)-1}) \neq \alpha_0 \cdots \alpha_j$.

Definition 7.3 Projection. Let X_0 and X_1 be two distributed algorithms. Let γ be a configuration of $X_0 \circ X_1$. The X_i-*projection* $\gamma_{|X_i}$ (with $i \in \{0, 1\}$) is the configuration of X_i obtained by removing from γ the values of all variables that do not exist in X_i.

Let $e = \gamma_0 \cdots \gamma_j \cdots$ be a sequence of configurations of $X_0 \circ X_1$. By extension, we also call X_i-*projection* the sequence of configurations $\gamma_{0|X_i} \cdots \gamma_{j|X_i} \cdots$ (with $i \in \{0, 1\}$).

By definitions of the composition and the projection, we have the following property.

Remark 7.4   Let A and B be two distributed algorithms. Let γ be a configuration of $B \circ A$. Let p be a process. Let R be an action of $A(p)$. If R is enabled (w.r.t. A) in $\gamma_{|A}$, then R is enabled (w.r.t. $(B \circ A)(p)$) in γ.

Notice that the previous property cannot be extended to Algorithm B, because of the local priorities. The following technical lemma will be used in the proof of Lemma 7.8.

Lemma 7.5   *Let A be a distributed algorithm that is silent in the network G under a distributed weakly fair daemon. Let B be a distributed algorithm such that no variable written by B appears in A. Let e be any execution of $B \circ A$ in G under a distributed weakly fair daemon. Then, $e' = \mathcal{MRS}(e_{|A})$ is a finite distributed weakly fair execution of A in G.*

Proof. We first show that e' is an execution of A in G.

Claim I: *All configurations of e' are possible configurations of A.*

Proof of the claim: By definition of the A-projection.

Claim II: *For every two consecutive configurations α and α' of e', we have $\alpha \overset{A}{\underset{G}{\mapsto}} \alpha'$.*

Proof of the claim: First, $\alpha \neq \alpha'$ by definition of the minimal relevant subsequence. Then, by Claim I and since no variable of A is written by B, every variable whose value is different between α and α' has been necessarily modified using actions of A in e. Finally, still by definition of the minimal relevant subsequence, all these modifications happen in a single step of A since, otherwise, α and α' would not be consecutive in e'.

Claim III: *If e' is finite, then the last configuration α_t of e' is a terminal configuration of A.*

Proof of the claim: By Claim I, α_t is a configuration of A. Assume, by contradiction, that α_t is not a terminal configuration of A. If e is finite, then its last configuration γ_t is terminal w.r.t. $B \circ A$. So, $\gamma_{t|A} = \alpha_t$ is a terminal configuration of A, a contradiction. Thus, e is infinite. Now the fact that e is infinite and e' is finite implies that there is an infinite suffix $s = \gamma_i \cdots$ of e such that $\gamma_{i|A} = \alpha_t$, for every i. In particular, no variable of A is modified in s despite α_t is not terminal. So, there is an action of A that is enabled at some process p in α_t which is continuously enabled w.r.t. $B \circ A$ all along s (Remark 7.4). Now, as e is weakly fair and $A(p)$ has priority over $B(p)$, p eventually modifies variables of $A(p)$ in s, and so in e, by executing an action of $A(p)$, a contradiction. Hence, α_t is a terminal configuration of A.

By Claims I-III, e' is an execution of A in G.

We now show that e' is distributed weakly fair. Consider now any processor p continuously enabled w.r.t. A from some configuration α of e'. Then, p is continuously enabled to execute an action of A from the first configuration of e that provides α (Remark 7.4), thus p eventually executes an action of A in e since e is weakly fair and $A(p)$ has priority over $B(p)$. Consequently, from α, p eventually executes an action of A in e' too. Hence, e' is a distributed weakly fair execution.

Finally, e' is finite since A is silent in G under a distributed weakly fair daemon. $\qquad\square$

Lemma 7.6 *Let* A *be a distributed algorithm that is silent in a network G under a distributed weakly fair daemon. Let* B *be a distributed algorithm such that no variable written by* B *appears in* A. *Let* $e = \gamma_0 \cdots \gamma_i \cdots$ *be any a distributed weakly fair execution of* $B \circ A$ *in G. Let the execution* $e' = \mathcal{MRS}(e_{|A}) = \alpha_0 \cdots \alpha_i \cdots$ *If* e' *contains R rounds, then* $\gamma_0 \cdots \gamma_T$, *where γ_T is the first configuration of e that provides the terminal configuration of e', contains at most R rounds.*

Proof. First, by Lemma 7.5, e' is a finite execution, so the integer R is defined. If $R = 0$, e' consists of a single configuration. Consequently, $\gamma_0 = \gamma_T$, and we are done. So, assume that $R > 0$. To prove the lemma in this case, we show, by induction, that $\forall i \in \{1, \ldots, R\}$, if e contains at least i rounds, then the ith round of e terminates at the earliest in $\gamma_{\zeta(R_i)}$, where α_{R_i} is the last configuration of the ith round of e'. (Recall that $\gamma_{\zeta(R_i)}$ denotes the first configuration of e that provides α_{R_i}.)

Base Case: If $i = 1$, then the first configuration of e' is not terminal and consequently the first configuration of e is not terminal either. Hence, e contains at least one round. Let $\alpha_0 \cdots \alpha_{R_1}$ be the first round of e'. By definition, there is a process p that is continuously enabled without executing any action of A in $\alpha_0 \cdots \alpha_{R_1-1}$. So, since $A(p)$ has priority over $B(p)$, p is continuously enabled without executing any action of $B \circ A$ in $\gamma_0 \cdots \gamma_{\zeta(R_1)-1}$ (Remark 7.4). Consequently, the first round of e terminates at the earliest in $\gamma_{\zeta(R_1)}$ and we are done.

Induction Hypothesis: Let k such that $1 \le k < R$. Assume the induction holds for $i = k$.

Induction Step: Assume that e contains at least $k + 1$ rounds. Since $k + 1 \le R$, e' contains at least $k + 1$ rounds too. So, let α_{R_k} and $\alpha_{R_{k+1}}$ be the last configurations of the kth and $k + 1^{th}$ rounds of e', respectively. By definition, α_{R_k} is also the first configuration the $k + 1^{th}$ rounds of e'. By definition again, there is a process p that is continuously enabled without executing any action of A in $\alpha_{R_k} \cdots \alpha_{R_{k+1}-1}$.

Since $A(p)$ has priority over $B(p)$, (*) p is continuously enabled without executing any action of $B \circ A$ in $\gamma_{\zeta(R_k)} \cdots \gamma_{\zeta(R_{k+1})-1}$. By induction hypothesis, Round k of e terminates, and so Round $k + 1$ of e starts, at the earliest in $\gamma_{\zeta(R_k)}$. If the round $k + 1$ of e starts in $\gamma_{\zeta(R_{k+1})}$

or after, we are done. Otherwise, Round $k + 1$ of e starts between $\gamma_{\zeta(R_k)}$ and $\gamma_{\zeta(R_{k+1})-1}$ (included), but cannot end before $\gamma_{\zeta(R_{k+1})}$ by (*), and we are done.

To conclude, if e contains less than R rounds, then the lemma immediately holds. Otherwise, the terminal configuration of e' is the last configuration of its Rth round and, from the induction, we can deduce that the Rth round of e terminates at the earliest in γ_T, i.e., $\gamma_0 \cdots \gamma_T$ contains at most R rounds.   □

We now define a particular class of specifications dedicated to composite algorithms.

Definition 7.7 X_i-Terminated.   Let X_0 and X_1 be two distributed algorithms. For every execution $e = \gamma_0 \cdots \gamma_j \cdots$ of $X_0 \circ X_1$, X_i-*Terminated*(e) holds (with $i \in \{0, 1\}$) if

1. $\gamma_{0|X_i}$ is a terminal configuration of X_i, and

2. $\gamma_{0|X_i} = \gamma_{k|X_i}$, $\forall k > 0$.

The following lemma shows that if an algorithm A is silent under a distributed weakly fair daemon, then, still assuming a distributed weakly fair daemon, any algorithm B, that does not write into the variables used by A, cannot prevent (even slow down) Algorithm A from reaching a terminal configuration in an execution of the composite algorithm B ∘ A.

Lemma 7.8   *Let A be a distributed algorithm that is silent in a network G under a distributed weakly fair daemon. Let B be a distributed algorithm such that no variable written by B appears in A.*

1. *Algorithm B ∘ A is self-stabilizing for A-Terminated in G under a distributed weakly fair daemon.*

2. *Its stabilization time in rounds (for A-Terminated) is less than or equal to the number of rounds Algorithm A requires to reach a terminal configuration.*

Proof. Let $e = \gamma_0 \cdots \gamma_i \cdots$ be any execution of B ∘ A in G under a distributed weakly fair daemon. Let $\mathcal{L} = \{\gamma_j : \gamma_{j|A}$ is a terminal configuration of A$\}$. Since no variable written by B appears in A, $\mathcal{L}$ is closed by B ∘ A and A-*Terminated* is satisfied from $\mathcal{L}$. We now show the convergence property. Let $e' = \mathcal{MRS}(e_{|A})$. By Lemma 7.5, e' is a finite distributed weakly fair execution of A in G. So, e' terminates within a finite number of rounds, say R. By Lemma 7.6, this, in turn, implies that e reaches within at most R rounds a configuration γ_j such that $\gamma_{j|A}$ is a terminal configuration of A, i.e., $\gamma_j \in \mathcal{L}$.   □

In Theorem 7.12 (the proposed sufficient condition), we use the property of (simple) silent stabilization, which is weaker than silent self-stabilization (see Remark 7.10).

Definition 7.9   Silent Stabilization.   Let A be a distributed algorithm, G be a network, D be a daemon, SP be a specification and Φ be a predicate over configurations. Algorithm A *silently stabilizes for Φ from SP in G under D* if

1. every execution e of Algorithm A in G under D such that $SP(e)$ holds is finite, and

2. every terminal configuration of every execution e of A such that $SP(e)$ holds satisfies Φ.

Remark 7.10 Let A be a distributed algorithm, G be a network, D be a daemon, SP be a specification and Φ be a predicate over configurations.

- If A is silent and self-stabilizing for Φ in G under D, then A silently stabilizes for Φ from SP in G under D.

- A is silent and self-stabilizing for Φ in G under D if and only if A silently stabilizes for Φ from *true* in G under D.

Our sufficient condition (Theorem 7.12 below) uses the notion of Φ-Fixed specification, defined below.

Definition 7.11 Φ-**Fixed.** Let Φ be a predicate over configurations. An execution $e = \gamma_0 \cdots \gamma_i \cdots$ is Φ-*Fixed* if

- $\Phi(\gamma_0)$ holds and

- all variables involved into Φ are constant all along e.

Notice that the X_i-Terminated specification is a particular instance of Φ-Fixed. From Lemma 7.8, we can deduce the following theorem.

Theorem 7.12 *Let A and B be two distributed algorithms. Let G be a network. Let SP_1 and SP_2 be two configuration predicates. Let Φ be a predicate over the variables common to A and B. Assume the following four conditions hold.*

1. *No variable written by B appears in A.*

2. *A is a silent and self-stabilizing for SP_1 in G under a distributed weakly fair daemon;*

3. *Φ holds in every terminal configuration of A, and*

4. *B silently stabilizes for SP_2 from Φ-Fixed in G under a distributed weakly fair daemon.*

Then,

- *B ∘ A is silent and self-stabilizing for $SP_1 \wedge SP_2$ in G under a distributed weakly fair daemon; and*

- *the stabilization time of* B ∘ A *is at most* $R_A + R_B$ *rounds, where* R_A *is the stabilization time in rounds of* A *and* R_B *is the maximum number of rounds that* B *requires to silently stabilize for* SP_2 *from* Φ*-Fixed in G.*

Proof. By Conditions 1 and 2, Lemma 7.8 applies: B ∘ A is self-stabilizing for A-Terminated in G under a distributed weakly fair daemon and its stabilization time in rounds is less than or equal to R_A. Notice that, by definition, A-Terminated(e) implies SP_1-fixed(e) for every execution (and so every suffix of execution) e of B ∘ A. Then, by Condition 3, (*) A-*Terminated(e) implies* Φ*-fixed(e) for every execution e of* B ∘ A. So, B ∘ A is also self-stabilizing for Φ-fixed ∧ SP_1-fixed in G under a distributed weakly fair daemon, still with a stabilization time of at most R_A rounds. Finally, since A is no more enabled in a suffix satisfying A-Terminated, B ∘ A also silently stabilizes for SP_2, within at most R_B additional rounds, from A-Terminated in G under a distributed weakly fair daemon by Condition 4 and (*), and we are done. □

Since Φ is a predicate over the variables common to A and B, Condition 1 implies that

- all variables involved into Φ are inputs in B (i.e., variables that may be read, but are never written by B). Such inputs maybe inputs from the system or computed by A, i.e., outputs from A; and

- consequently, for every execution $e = \gamma_0 \cdots$ of B, we have $\Phi(\gamma_0)$ if and only if Φ-Fixed(e).

Finally, notice that the sufficient condition proposed in Theorem 7.12 can be further extended to show the self-stabilization (maybe not silent) of a composite algorithm under a distributed weakly fair daemon by modifying Condition 4. However, it seems to be difficult to remove the silent condition on A in Condition 2.

7.2   A TOY EXAMPLE

The following case study underlines how important spanning tree constructions are in the self-stabilizing area. Roughly speaking, many self-stabilizing algorithms can be summed up as "first construct a spanning tree, then solve your problem using convergecast and/or broadcast communications along the tree."

Assume the network $G = (V, E)$ is connected and rooted at some process r. Also assume that every process p has a constant integer input $p.In$. Finally, consider a distributed weakly fair daemon. Our goal is to provide a self-stabilizing and silent (composite) algorithm COMPO that computes in the output integer variable $p.Out$ of every process p the maximum value over all the inputs. Thus, each terminal configuration of COMPO should satisfy the predicate

$$P_{\max} \stackrel{\text{def}}{=} \forall p \in V, p.Out = \max_{q \in V} q.In.$$

COMPO actually consists of the composition of three sub-algorithms.

1. The first sub-algorithm is a silent and self-stabilizing spanning tree construction. Here, we will use Algorithm BFS presented in Chapter 5.

2. Once the first sub-algorithm has stabilized, the second sub-algorithm, called STM (stands for *Sub-Tree Maximum*), stabilizes to a configuration from which each process p stores in a variable $p.maxDesc$ the maximum over the inputs of its descendents in the tree. This algorithm is implemented as a convergecast toward the root.

3. Once the two first sub-algorithms have stabilized, the third sub-algorithm, called INMAX (stands for *Input Maximum*), stabilizes to terminal configuration where each process p stores in $p.Out$ the maximum over the all inputs, i.e., where $P_{\max}$ holds. This latter sub-algorithm simply consists in broadcasting the value of $r.maxDesc$ into all outputs Out, since the set of all root's descendents in the tree is exactly V.

Hence, we define our composite algorithm as COMPO = INMAX ∘ STM ∘ BFS. We now give more details about each layer.

Notice that, following the algorithmic approach 1 presented in page 89, Algorithms STM and INMAX are actually algorithms designed for oriented tree topologies.

7.2.1   ALGORITHM BFS

Recall that Algorithm BFS is silent and self-stabilizing in G (see Chapter 5). In each of its terminal configuration, its variables describe a (BFS) spanning tree rooted at r, i.e., every terminal configuration of BFS satisfies predicate *BFST* (see page 48 for its definition). Moreover, the computed tree is *oriented* toward the root: each non-root process p designates its parent in the tree using the pointer $p.par$. Conversely, a process q is a *child* of p if and only if p is the parent of q in the tree. We denote by $Children(p)$ the set of all p's children in the tree.

To implement a convergecast along the tree, each process needs to determine its children in the tree among its neighbors in G using available information.

Since the tree computed by Algorithm BFS is breadth-first, all neighbors of the root r are its *children*, i.e.,

$$Children(r) = r.\mathcal{N}.$$

Let p be any non-root process. Using the variables of BFS, p can determine its children as follows. A neighbor q of p is its children if (1) $q \neq r$ and (2) $q.par$ designates p as the parent of q. Process p can easily test whether q is the root, since in any terminal configuration of BFS, r is the only process with a distance variable d equal to 0. Hence, the subset of non-root neighbors of p, $\mathcal{N}^\star(p)$, is defined as follows:

$$\mathcal{N}^\star(p) = \{q \in p.\mathcal{N} \; : \; q.d \neq 0\}.$$

Condition (2) is more intricate. Indeed, if $q \neq r$, then $q.par \in q.\mathcal{N}$, where $q.\mathcal{N}$ is a set of *local labels* that indirectly designate each of its neighbors. So, p should be able to test whether the local label contained in $q.par$ designates it. Following [CD94], we assume that each process p can identify its local label in the set $q.\mathcal{N}$ of each of its neighbors q using the function α_p, i.e., the local label designating p in $q.\mathcal{N}$ is $\alpha_p(q)$, for every $q \in p.\mathcal{N}$.[1] Hence,

$$Children(p) = \{q \in \mathcal{N}^\star(p) \; : \; q.par = \alpha_p(q)\}.$$

Any process that has no child is called a *leaf*. The set of *descendents* of any process p is recursively defined as follows: any leaf has only one descendent, itself; and the descendents of any non-leaf process p is the union of the singleton $\{p\}$ and the sets of descendents of all its children. The *subtree* of any process p in an oriented tree T, noted $T(p)$, is the subgraph induced by the set of its descendents in T. In the following, by a slight abuse of notation, we identify any subtree $T(p)$ by the set of its nodes, i.e., the descendents of p. The *height* of a process p, noted $h(p)$, is recursively defined as follows: $h(p) = 0$ if p is a leaf, $h(p) = 1 + \max_{q \in Children(p)} h(q)$ otherwise. Let $H = h(r)$ be the height of T. Recall that, in a terminal configuration of BFS, the computed tree satisfies $H \leq D$. The *level* of a process p, $lvl(p)$, in an oriented tree is recursively defined as follows: $lvl(p) = 0$ if $p = r$, $lvl(p) = lvl(q) + 1$ where q is the parent of p otherwise.

Since the distributed weakly fair daemon is stronger that the distributed unfair daemon, Theorems 5.13 (page 54) and 5.18 (page 57) imply the following result.

Theorem 7.13   *Algorithm BFS is silent and self-stabilizing for configuration predicate BFST (i.e., the BFS spanning tree construction specification) in every connected rooted network under the distributed weakly fair daemon. Its stabilization time is at most $D + 2$ rounds.*

Let $\mathcal{T} = (V_T, E_T)$ where $V_T = V$ and $E_T = \{\{p, q\} \in E \; : \; q \in Children(p)\}$. Let $\Phi_{\text{BFS}}(\gamma)$ be the predicate over variables of BFS that holds if $\mathcal{T}$ is a BFS spanning tree rooted at r. By definition of *BFST*, Remark 7.14 follows.

Remark 7.14 Φ_{BFS} holds in every terminal configuration of BFS.

7.2.2   ALGORITHM STM

Algorithm STM, whose code is given in Algorithm 7.7, consists of a single bottom-up action per process: Action *Cnv*.

We now show that Algorithm STM ∘ BFS is silent and self-stabilizing for the configuration predicate P_{STM} (defined below) in every connected rooted network under the distributed weakly fair daemon:

$$P_{STM} \stackrel{\text{def}}{=} \forall p \in V, p.maxDesc = \max\{q.In \; : \; q \in \mathcal{T}(p)\},$$

where $\mathcal{T}$ is the BFS spanning tree computed by BFS.

---

[1] This assumption is not a restriction. Indeed it can be easily implemented in real message passing systems: each process q just has to regularly send to each neighbor p its local label designating p, i.e., the value of $\alpha_p(q)$. By storing the latest received information from each neighbor q, p eventually "knows" that q designates it with $\alpha_p(q)$.

Algorithm 7.7 Algorithm STM, code for each process p

Inputs:
$p.In \in \mathbb{N}$:   input from the system
All variables of Algorithm BFS(p)

Variable:
$p.maxDesc \in \mathbb{N}$

Macros:

$$
\begin{aligned}
\mathcal{N}^{\star}(p) \quad &= \quad \{q \in p.\mathcal{N} \,:\, q.d \neq 0\} \\
Children(p) \quad &= \quad p.\mathcal{N} \text{ if } p = r, \{q \in \mathcal{N}^{\star}(p) \,:\, q.par = \alpha_p(q)\} \text{ otherwise} \\
MaxST(p) \quad &= \quad \max(\{p.In\} \cup \{q.maxDesc \,:\, q \in Children(p)\})
\end{aligned}
$$

Predicate:

$$
UpdateMST(p) \quad \overset{\text{def}}{=} \quad p.maxDesc \neq MaxST(p)
$$

Action:

$$
Cnv \quad :: \quad UpdateMST(p) \quad \rightarrow \quad p.maxDesc \leftarrow MaxST(p)
$$

From the respective codes of Algorithm STM and Algorithm BFS (page 49), Remark 7.15 follows.

Remark 7.15   No variable written by STM appears in BFS.

Remark that, since all variables of BFS are inputs in STM, Φ_{BFS} is actually a predicate over the variables common to BFS and STM. Then, by Theorem 7.13 and Remarks 7.14 and 7.15, the first three conditions of Theorem 7.12 hold, and it remains to show that STM silently stabilizes for P_{STM} from Φ_{BFS}-Fixed in every connected rooted network under a distributed weakly fair daemon.

Lemma 7.16   *P_{STM} holds in any terminal configuration of* STM *satisfying* Φ_{BFS}.

Proof. Let γ_t be any terminal configuration of STM satisfying Φ_{BFS}. We show, by induction of the heights of processes in $\mathcal{T}$, that $\gamma_t(p).maxDest = \max_{q \in \mathcal{T}(p)}\{q.In\}$, for every process p.

Base case: Let p be any process such that $h(p) = 0$ in γ_t. By definition, p is a leaf, i.e., $Children(p) = \emptyset$. Thus, $MaxST(p) = p.In$. Now, since Action Cnv is disabled at p in γ_t, we have $\gamma_t(p).maxDest = p.In$. Moreover, since p is a leaf, $\mathcal{T}(p) = \{p\}$. Hence, $\max_{q \in \mathcal{T}(p)}\{q.In\} = p.In = \gamma_t(p).maxDest$, and we are done.

Induction Hypothesis: Let $k \geq 0$. Assume that for every process p such that $h(p) \leq k$, we have $\gamma_t(p).maxDest = \max_{q \in \mathcal{T}(p)}\{q.In\}$.

Induction Step: Let p be a process such that $h(p) = k + 1$. By definition, $\mathcal{T}(p) = \{p\} \cup \bigcup_{c \in Children(p)} \mathcal{T}(c)$. By induction hypothesis, $\forall c \in Children(p)$, $\gamma_t(c).maxDest = \max_{q \in \mathcal{T}(c)}\{q.In\}$. Now, since Action Cnv is disabled at p in γ_t, we deduce that, in γ_t, $p.maxDest = MaxST(p) = \max(\{p.In\} \cup \{c.maxDesc : c \in Children(p)\}) = \max(\{p.In\} \cup \bigcup_{c \in Children(p)} \max_{q \in \mathcal{T}(c)}\{q.In\}) = \max_{q \in \mathcal{T}(p)}\{q.In\}$, and we are done.

By letting $k = H$, the lemma holds. □

Lemma 7.17   *Every Φ_{BFS}–Fixed execution e of* STM *converges within at most $\mathcal{D} + 1$ rounds to a terminal configuration.*

Proof. We show by induction on the heights of processes in $\mathcal{T}$ that each process p is disabled forever after at most $h(p) + 1$ rounds. Since $\mathcal{T}$ is breadth-first, $H \leq \mathcal{D}$ and so the lemma immediately follows.

Base case: Let p be any process such that $h(p) = 0$ in γ_t. By definition, p is a leaf, i.e., $Children(p) = \emptyset$. Thus, $MaxST(p) = p.In$.

If $p.maxDest = p.In$, then p is disabled forever because $p.In$ is a constant input.

Otherwise, p is continuously enabled until it executes Action Cnv since the guard of Cnv (the only action of STM) only depends on $p.maxDest$ and the constant $p.In$. Hence, within at most one round, p executes Action Cnv and we retrieve the previous case.

So, p is disabled forever within at most one round, and we are done.

Induction Hypothesis: Let $k \geq 0$. Assume that for every process p such that $h(p) \leq k$, p is disabled forever after at most $h(p) + 1$ rounds.

Induction Step: Let p be a process such that $h(p) = k + 1$. At the end of the $k + 1^{th}$ round, the value of $\{q.maxDesc : q \in Children(p)\}$ is constant forever, by induction hypothesis. Thus, from that point the guard of Cnv (the only action of STM) only depends on $p.maxDest$ and constant variables. Hence, as in the base case, within at most one additional round, p is disabled forever, and we are done.

□

By Lemmas 7.17 and 7.16, Theorem 7.18 follows.

Theorem 7.18   *Within at most $\mathcal{D} + 1$ rounds,* STM *silently stabilizes for P_{STM} from Φ_{BFS}–Fixed in every connected rooted network under a distributed weakly fair daemon.*

Algorithm 7.8 Algorithm INMAX, code for the root process r.

Inputs:
All variables of Algorithm $(\text{STM} \circ \text{BFS})(p)$

Variable:
$r.Out \in \mathbb{N}$

Action:
$Brd \quad :: \quad r.Out \neq r.maxDesc \quad \rightarrow \quad r.Out \leftarrow r.maxDesc$

Algorithm 7.9 Algorithm INMAX, code for the any non-root process p

Inputs:
All variables of Algorithm $(\text{STM} \circ \text{BFS})(p)$

Variable:
$p.Out \in \mathbb{N}$

Action:
$Brd \quad :: \quad p.Out \neq p.par.Out \quad \rightarrow \quad p.Out \leftarrow p.par.Out$

By Remarks 7.15 and 7.14, and Theorems 7.12, 7.13, and 7.18, Theorem 7.19 follows.

Theorem 7.19   STM $\circ$ BFS *is silent and self-stabilizing for BFST $\wedge P_{STM}$ in every connected rooted network under the distributed weakly fair daemon. Its stabilization time is at most $2\mathcal{D} + 3$ rounds.*

7.2.3   ALGORITHM INMAX

Algorithm INMAX, whose code is given in Algorithms 7.8 and 7.9, is semi-anonymous and consists of a single top-down action per process: Action *Brd*.

We now show that Algorithm COMPO = INMAX $\circ$ STM $\circ$ BFS is silent and self-stabilizing for configuration predicate $P_{\max}$ (actually *BFST* $\wedge P_{STM} \wedge P_{\max}$) in every connected rooted network under the distributed weakly fair daemon.

From the respective codes of INMAX and the composite algorithm STM $\circ$ BFS, Remark 7.20 follows.

Remark 7.20   No variable written by INMAX appears in STM $\circ$ BFS.

Let

$$\Phi_{\text{STM}}(\gamma) \stackrel{\text{def}}{=} \Phi_{\text{BFS}}(\gamma) \wedge P_{\text{STM}}(\gamma).$$

Remark that, since all variables of STM ∘ BFS are inputs in INMAX, Φ_{STM} is actually a predicate over the variables common to STM ∘ BFS and INMAX. Moreover, by Remark 7.14 and Lemma 7.16, Remark 7.21 follows.

Remark 7.21 Φ_{STM} holds in every terminal configuration of STM ∘ BFS.

Thus, to apply Theorem 7.12, it remains to show that INMAX silently stabilizes for P_{max} from Φ_{STM}-Fixed in every connected rooted network under a distributed weakly fair daemon.

Lemma 7.22 P_{max} holds in any terminal configuration of INMAX satisfying Φ_{STM}.

Proof. Let γ_t be any terminal configuration of INMAX satisfying Φ_{STM}. We show, by induction on the levels of processes in $\mathcal{T}$, that $\gamma_t(p).Out = \max_{q \in V} q.In$, for every process p.

Base case: By definition, the root r is the unique process at level 0 in γ_t. Now, since Action *Brd* is disabled at r in γ_t, we have $\gamma_t(r).Out = \gamma_t(r).maxDesc$. Now, by definition of Φ_{STM}, $\gamma_t(r).maxDesc = \max_{q \in \mathcal{T}(r)}\{q.In\} = \max_{q \in V} q.In$, since $\mathcal{T}(r)$ spans G. Hence, $\gamma_t(r).Out = \gamma_t(r).maxDesc = \max_{q \in V} q.In$, and we are done.

Induction Hypothesis: Let $k \geq 0$. Assume that for every process p such that $lvl(p) \leq k$, we have $\gamma_t(p).Out = \max_{q \in V} q.In$.

Induction Step: Let p be a process such that $lvl(p) = k + 1$. Then, since $lvl(p) = k + 1 > 0$, $p \neq r$. By induction hypothesis, its parent x (such that $lvl(x) = k$) satisfies $\gamma_t(x).Out = \max_{q \in V} q.In$. Now, since Action *Brd* is disabled at $p \neq r$ in γ_t, $\gamma_t(p).Out = \gamma_t(p).par.Out = \gamma_t(x).Out = \max_{q \in V} q.In$, and we are done.

By letting $k = H$, the lemma holds.   □

Lemma 7.23   Every Φ_{STM}-Fixed execution e of INMAX converges within at most $\mathcal{D} + 1$ rounds to a terminal configuration.

Proof. We show by induction on the levels of processes in $\mathcal{T}$ that each process p is disabled forever after at most $lvl(p) + 1$ rounds. Since $\mathcal{T}$ is breadth-first, the maximum level of a process is less than or equal to $\mathcal{D}$ and so the lemma immediately follows.

Base case: By definition, the root r is the unique process at level 0 in γ_t.

If $r.Out = r.maxDesc$, r is disabled forever because $r.maxDesc$ is a constant (e satisfies Φ_{STM}).

Otherwise, r is continuously enabled until it executes Action Brd since the guard of Brd (the only action of INMAX) only depends on $r.Out$ and the constant $r.maxDesc$. Hence, within at most one round r executes Action Brd and we retrieve the previous case.

So, r is disabled forever within at most one round, and we are done.

Induction Hypothesis: Let $k \geq 0$. Assume that for every process p such that $lvl(p) \leq k$, p is disabled forever after at most $lvl(p) + 1$ rounds.

Induction Step: Let p be a process such that $lvl(p) = k + 1$. At the end of the $k + 1^{th}$ round, the value of $p.par.Out$ is constant forever, by induction hypothesis. Thus, from that point the guard of Brd (the only action of INMAX) only depends on $p.Out$ and the constant variable $p.par.Out$. Hence, as in the base case, within at most one additional round, p is disabled forever, and we are done.

$\square$

By Lemmas 7.23 and 7.22, follows.

Theorem 7.24   *Within at most $\mathcal{D} + 1$ rounds*, INMAX *silently stabilizes for $P_{\max}$ from Φ_{STM}-Fixed in every connected rooted network under a distributed weakly fair daemon.*

By Remarks 7.20, 7.21, and Theorems 7.13, 7.19, and 7.24, Theorem 7.25 follows.

Theorem 7.25   COMPO = INMAX ∘ STM ∘ BFS *is silent and self-stabilizing for $BFST \wedge P_{\text{STM}} \wedge P_{\max}$ in every connected rooted network under the distributed weakly fair daemon. Its stabilization time is at most $3\mathcal{D} + 4$ rounds.*

In Figure 7.1, we present a synchronous execution of Algorithm COMPO. Starting from Configuration (i), the execution reaches a terminal configuration in 9 rounds, according to Theorem 7.25 which gives a bound of at most ten rounds in this case. In details, Algorithm BFS stabilizes in the first three rounds. The actual convergence of Algorithm STM then starts in configuration (iv) and also lasts three rounds. Finally, the actual convergence of Algorithm INMAX starts in configuration (vii) and also consists of three rounds, leading to the terminal configuration: Configuration (x).

7.3   HIERARCHICAL VS. NONHIERARCHICAL COLLATERAL COMPOSITION

We have motivated the hierarchical variant of the collateral composition by the fact that the (nonhierarchical) collateral composition of Herman [Her92b] may introduce nondeterminism in the execution of the sub-algorithms.

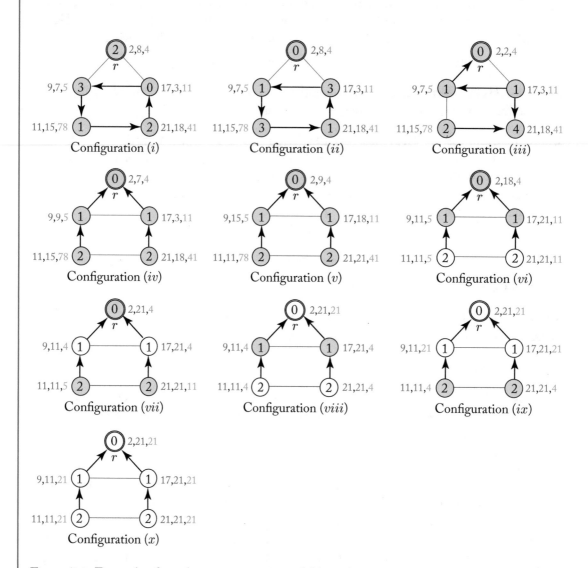

Figure 7.1: Example of synchronous execution of Algorithm COMPO = INMAX ∘ STM ∘ BFS, with $D = 4 > \mathcal{D} = 2$: the double-circled node is the root, the arrow from node p to node q indicates that p designates q as its parent using $p.par$, values of variable d are given inside the nodes, numbers close to the nodes, respectively, give the values of $p.In$ (in red), $p.maxDesc$ (in blue), and $p.Out$ (in green). Enabled nodes are filled in gray.

Local nondeterminism in action executions may lead to inefficient solutions. For example, it is proven in [DJ16] that the silent BFS algorithm proposed by Huang and Chen [HC92] has a stabilization time in $\Omega(n)$ rounds (where n is the number of processes). This lower bound is due to the fact that the proposed algorithm consists of two non locally mutually exclusive actions. Indeed, it is also shown in [DJ16] that solving this nondeterminism using the appropriate local priorities leads to a solution asymptotically optimal in rounds (i.e., $O(\mathcal{D})$).

Notice also that the absence of any local priority may introduce nondeterminism that can even lead to non-stabilizing solutions under the distributed weakly fair daemon. If we compose Algorithms INMAX, STM, and BFS using the (nonhierarchical) collateral composition of Herman [Her92b], then actions of INMAX, STM, and BFS may be simultaneously enabled at the same process. In this case, the daemon may activate any of the enabled actions. In Figure 7.2, we propose a synchronous execution (and so a particular case of distributed weakly fair execution) of the (nonhierarchical) collateral composition of INMAX, STM, and BFS, where the daemon preferably chooses to execute INMAX, then STM, and finally BFS. Notice that this execution starts from the same initial configuration as the one presented in Figure 7.1. Moreover, this execution is made possible by the absence of local priorities: in such a case, the daemon is allowed to apply any kind of priority. These adversarial choices actually lead to a non-terminating execution. Indeed, one can remark that Configurations (v) and (ix) are identical.

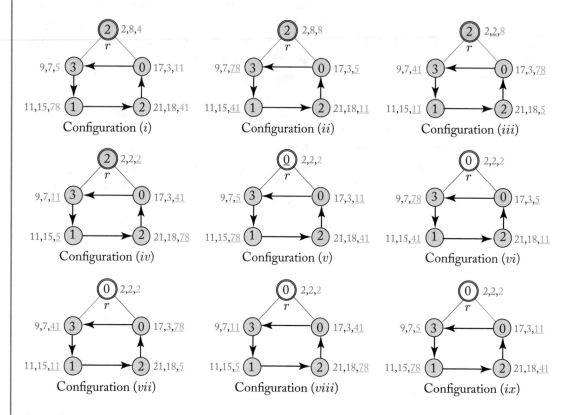

Figure 7.2: Fragment of synchronous non-stabilizing execution using the (non-hierarchical) collateral composition of Herman [Her92b]. The new value of each variable modified in a step $\gamma_i \mapsto \gamma_{i+1}$ is underlined in γ_{i+1}.

CHAPTER 8

Self-Stabilization in Message Passing Systems

Previous chapters were dedicated to self-stabilization in the abstract atomic-state model. At the opposite side, the message passing model is the closest from real-life networks. This chapter is a quick introduction to the design of self-stabilizing algorithms in message passing systems. In Section 8.1, we briefly present the message passing model. In Section 8.2, we review literature about self-stabilization in message passing systems. The next two sections give hints to implement self-stabilizing algorithms in message passing: Section 8.3 deals with silent algorithms, while Section 8.4 deals with dynamic specifications. In the last section, we discuss about the problem of evaluating stabilization time in message passing.

8.1 MESSAGE PASSING FOR SELF-STABILIZING SYSTEMS

Numerous variations of message passing models have been proposed in the self-stabilizing area. Here, we introduce the main features that have to be characterized to obtain an operational model. Moreover, we state the common assumptions made in the use cases presented in this chapter.

8.1.1 COMMUNICATION LINKS

In message passing, neighboring processes can exchange information through messages sent in an intermediate communication medium, called *link* or *channel*. This latter allows to formalize a physical wire in a wired network, for example. As for previous chapters, we recall that we consider distributed systems where communication links are bidirectional, i.e., the directed link (p, q) exists if and only if the directed link (q, p) exists.

To use such a communication medium, each process has two communication primitives, one for sending messages in a link, the other for receiving messages from a link. Each reception is preceded by a delivery: a message is delivered as soon as it is available to be received, precisely as soon as it is stored in a dedicated buffer in the local memory of the receiver. In the self-stabilizing context, the reception primitive has to be *non-blocking*: in absence of any delivered message, the call to the reception function terminates, yet by returning a value notifying the absence of any received message. This is mandatory to prevent deadlock, e.g., two neighboring processes waiting for a message from each other, while the link is initially empty.

Another important feature is the order of messages in a link, which may be *FIFO* (First In First Out) or arbitrary. FIFO means that in each directed link (p, q), the order in reception at q follows the order of message sending at p. Real physical links are inherently FIFO. However, in some systems such as peer-to-peer systems, links between neighbors are actually logical rather than physical, i.e., they represent the ability of communicating, through a path maintained by a routing protocol, between processes, maybe arbitrarily far from each other. Such routing paths may be updated from time to time to self-adapt to faults or traffic load, justifying then the possibility of message reordering.

The reliability of the links should be also characterized. The link reliability is usually defined as the conjunction of the following three properties.

No Creation: A message can be received by process p from its neighbor q only if it has been sent by process q before.

No Loss: Any message sent by process q to its neighbor p is eventually delivered to process p.

No Duplication: Each message is delivered at most once.

In the use cases, we assume that links do not suffer from any message duplication. However, due to the arbitrary initial configuration, links may initially contain a finite, yet (maybe) unbounded, number of (correctly formatted but) arbitrary valued messages.[1] Now, except for these initial messages, links do not suffer from any further message creation. Hence, a message can be received by process p from its neighbor q only if it has been sent by process q before or if it was initially in the link (q, p). In our case studies, messages may be lost. However, we assume that the links are *fair lossy* [BCT96]: if infinitely many messages are sent by process q to process p, then infinitely many messages are delivered to p, i.e., infinitely many messages are received by p, provided that p regularly invokes its reception primitive to receive these messages.[2] Notice that the fair loss of messages is a kind of *intermittent failure*, such impermanent failures are characterized by a frequency of occurrence higher than that of transient faults. So, under such failure patterns, the convergence of self-stabilizing algorithm should be effective even while such faults continue to occur in the system.

Finally, links are assumed to be *asynchronous*: if not lost, a message in a link is delivered in a finite, yet unbounded, time.

8.1.2   PROCESS EXECUTION

In message passing systems, the (local) code of processes is usually organized as follows: each process first tries to receive some messages, then updates its own state (according to the re-

---

[1]Recall that, it is commonly assumed that any message is still correctly formatted after transient faults, since otherwise the message can be simply discarded.

[2]An example of fair lossy link is a link where each one in two consecutive messages is lost.

ceived information or the absence of reception), and finally sends messages to all or a part of its neighbors. Now, due to the arbitrary initialization, the three previous steps should be executed infinitely often to prevent deadlocks. Moreover, to prevent the system from any congestion, a process should regulate its message sending using timers, i.e., functions whose executions are triggered after some amount of time. It is worth noticing that, usually in the literature, there is no assumption on the periodicity of the timer triggering, except that it should happen infinitely often. Indeed, the processes are also assumed to be fair yet asynchronous: they execute infinitely many steps (*process fairness*), but the finite time between two of their consecutive steps is unbounded (asynchrony). Of course, each process can only send a finite number of messages per step (Zeno executions are forbidden).

8.1.3   CONFIGURATIONS OF THE SYSTEM

In the message passing model, information exchanges are explicit while in the two other classical models (i.e, atomic-state and register models), information exchanges are implicit since they are done using read and write operations on locally shared variables. An immediate consequence is a more complex definition of configuration in message passing. In this context, a configuration is defined as a vector of the states of each process and directed link. The state of a directed link consists in either the list or the multiset of messages it contains, depending on whether or not communications are assumed to be FIFO.

8.2   RELATED WORK

The *data-link* protocol is the fundamental basic tool to implement self-stabilizing algorithms in message passing systems. It is actually a synchronization protocol between two neighbors which aims at providing two high-level primitives (one for sending and the other for receiving) allowing to reliably transmit, in a FIFO manner, a data packet from a sender to a receiver over an unreliable (FIFO) channel. Notice that implementing self-stabilizing solutions for such a strong specification is a major issue. As a matter of fact, existing self-stabilizing data-link solutions implement a slightly weaker, yet practical, specification; see Section 8.4.2.

Self-stabilizing data-link protocols proposed in the literature are actually generalizations of the *alternating bit protocol* proposed by Lynch (ABP) [Lyn68]. Precisely, they are based on the same principles but, contrary to the ABP, they usually require more than two sequence numbers. The main idea is that, using messages tagged with those sequence numbers, a self-stabilizing data-link protocol will eventually flush the link of the spurious messages whose existence is inherently due to the arbitrary initialization of the system.

Gouda and Multari [GM91] have proposed a self-stabilizing (deterministic) data-link protocol which is basically an ABP that uses (unbounded) integers as sequence numbers. However, their solution requires infinite local memories at each process due to the use of such unbounded sequence numbers. Now, Gouda and Multari also show in the same paper that deterministic self-stabilization is impossible in message passing for a wide class of problems, including the data-link problem, using bounded process memories when the *link capacity*, i.e., the maximum number of messages that can be in transit at each instant in a directed link, cannot be bounded. This impossibility result has been further generalized by Dolev et al. [DIM97a], since they show that a wide class of dynamic problems, including token passing, have a self-stabilizing solution in message passing only if each execution of the solution algorithm on a finite network contains infinitely many distinct configurations.

Conversely, Varghese [Var00] proposed a technique called *counter flushing* to design several self-stabilizing deterministic protocols that use bounded sequence counters, and so bounded process memories, assuming the link capacity is bounded and such a bound is *a priori* known by all processes (an overview of his solution will be presented in Section 8.4). Awerbuch et al. justify the bounded link capacity assumption by claiming that "real links are inherently bounded anyway" [APVD94]. Notice that bounded links are usually considered unreliable, in which case any sending through an already full link necessarily fails. Notice also that Varghese rightly asserted that his method allows to easily implement a self-stabilizing deterministic data-link protocol that also uses bounded local memories. By the way, his method has been then successfully used in other papers to self-stabilizingly solve various problems, such as token circulation [PV00] or spanning tree constructions [AB98]. The work of Varghese [Var00] also includes a Propagation of Information with Feedback (PIF) protocol that can be used to implement reset and snapshot protocols. Even a snap-stabilizing PIF algorithm under the same setting is available in [LMV16].[3] So, the general transformer proposed by Katz and Perry [KP93], which is based on a reset and a snapshot algorithm, can be adapted so that it still works using bounded process memories, yet assuming bounded capacity links (see Section 8.4.5). This shows that the link capacity is central in the expressiveness of self-stabilization in message passing.

Notice that the orthogonal issues "bounded memories vs. unbounded link capacity" can be circumvented by considering weaker form of self-stabilization. Burns et al. [BGM93] show that the alternating bit protocol proposed by Lynch [Lyn68], i.e., a data-link protocol using two sequence values per processes, is actually *pseudo-stabilizing* in message passing systems with unbounded capacity links. The pseudo-stabilization and the self-stabilization differ by their closure property, indeed in pseudo-stabilization, closure is eventual since every execution should have a suffix satisfying the specification (yet the time to reach this suffix may be unboundable). Afek and Brown [AB93] have presented a *probabilistic* self-stabilizing data-link protocol, still assuming unbounded capacity links, that works using any bounded set of at least three sequence numbers. Probabilistic self-stabilization differs from deterministic self-stabilization by the convergence property, i.e., in probabilistic self-stabilization, the convergence is not certain since it is only guaranteed with probability one.[4]

---

[3]Recall that snap-stabilization is a stronger form of self-stabilization.

[4]In other words, *almost surely*, meaning that there may be non-converging executions, made as infinite sequences of illegitimate configurations, but given an arbitrary initial configuration, the probability that the execution does not converge is 0.

All the aforementioned literature considers FIFO links. Dubois et al. succeed in removing this assumption in [DDPT11]. Indeed, they proposed a self-stabilizing data-link protocol that uses a bounded number of sequence values working on non-FIFO bounded-capacity links. Moreover, after a careful check of the proofs, anyone can deduce that the FIFO assumption is useless in the unbounded solution proposed by Gouda and Multari [GM91].

Notice also that Dolev [Dol00] proposes a general method to translate any self-stabilizing protocol written in the atomic-state model into the register one, and then from the register model to the message passing model. The transformation requires the network to be connected, and either rooted or fully identified (the transformation for rooted networks is presented in Section 8.4.3). Moreover, in the transformation, the data-link protocol is an abstract black box. So, any of the previous data-link solutions can be used in this general method, yet with the required assumptions on the link capacity and process memory.

Finally, few papers [DDT06, APSV91] succeed in proposing self-stabilizing algorithms that uses bounded process memories in message passing without any additional assumption on the model, in particular on the link capacity. However, according to the impossibility result of Gouda and Multari [GM91], these solutions cannot be general. Awerbuch et al. [APSV91] introduced the property of *local correctability* and demonstrated that protocols which are locally correctable can be self-stabilized using bounded memory per process in spite of unbounded capacity links. Delaët et al. [DDT06] also proposed a method allowing to design silent self-stabilizing protocols with bounded memory per process in message passing systems equipped with unreliable links of unbounded capacity for a class of fixpoint problems, namely those that can be expressed in terms of *r-operators*, a particular algebra defined in their paper (an overview of this method will be presented in the next section). Notice that, until now, the exact class of problems that admit a self-stabilizing solution using bounded local memories yet assuming unbounded capacity links is still unknown.

8.3   A LIGHTWEIGHT TECHNIQUE FOR SILENT ALGORITHMS

In [DDT06], Delaët et al. propose a simple solution for designing particular silent self-stabilizing algorithms in message passing systems, namely those that can be expressed in terms of *r*-operators.

8.3.1   SILENCE IN MESSAGE PASSING

The notion of silence is quite different in message passing as compared to shared memory models. Indeed, to prevent deadlock, processes are required to send messages infinitely often. Hence, executions of silent algorithms in message passing cannot be finite.

Recall that silence is introduced in [DGS99] as follows: a silent self-stabilizing algorithm converges within finite time to a configuration from which the values of the *communication variables* used by the algorithm remain fixed. In message passing, a communication variable of process p is a buffer variable whose value is sent and/or received through messages. Therefore, a configuration γ is considered as *terminal* if the values of all communication variables are constant in all possible executions starting from γ. From such a configuration, information exchanged between processes is also fixed.

8.3.2   THE TRANSFORMER

The method proposed by Delaët et al. can be straightforwardly used to transform certain silent self-stabilizing algorithms written in the atomic-state model into the message passing model. Of course, the transformation preserves the specification of the input algorithm. The method tolerates fair lossy asynchronous links with any number of message reordering (i.e., links may not be FIFO).

The translation into message passing of an algorithm A written in the atomic-state model consists in the general pattern given below.

- Each process p maintains the following variables:

  - its variables in $A(p)$, and
  - an array $p.States[]$, indexed on $p.\mathcal{N}$, such that p stores in $p.States[q]$ a state of $A(q)$, for every $q \in p.\mathcal{N}$.

- The code of p is then divided into the following three statements.

  1. Using a timer, p regularly sends to all its neighbors its "current state in A", i.e., the projection of its local state on its A's variables.
  2. p stores in $p.States[q]$ the most recently received state from its neighbor q.
     To that goal, p regularly (i.e., using the previous timer or another one) calls the reception primitive to try receive a message from q, for each $q \in p.\mathcal{N}$.
     If the reception succeeds, then p updates $p.States[q]$ with the state stored in the received message.
  3. Regularly (i.e., using one of the two previous timers or another one), p checks the values of its A's variables and all states in $p.States[]$ to determine whether it is enabled in $A(p)$.
     If so, p updates its A's variables accordingly.

8.3.3   AN EXAMPLE

Consider Algorithm BFS presented in Chapter 5.

As processes are fair, each process p updates its state infinitely often according to its own state, the values in $p.States[]$, and the actions of $BFS(p)$. Consequently, from the actions of Algorithm BFS, we can deduce that eventually the distance variable of the root r, i.e., $r.d$, is fixed to 0 and the value of $p.d$ becomes forever greater than or equal to 1, for every non-root process p.

Since every message is eventually received or lost, eventually every neighbor of the root r only receives states from the root indicating that $r.d = 0$, while other non-root processes always receives states from their neighbors where the distance values are greater than or equal to 1. From that point, the next time processes will update their state (it will happen, as processes are fair), the value $p.d$ of every neighbor of the root will become fixed to 1 forever, while the variable $q.d$ of every other non-root process will become forever greater than or equal to 2. So on and so forth, we can then show by induction that $\forall k \geq 1$, the system gradually converges to configurations from which every process p forever satisfies:

- if $\|p, r\| < k$, then $p.d = \|p, r\|$,

- $p.d \geq k$ otherwise.

(The reasoning is actually similar to Lemma 5.14, page 55.) Hence, by letting $k = \mathcal{D} + 1$, we deduce that eventually the system reaches a configuration from which every process p satisfies $p.d = \|p, r\|$ forever. From such a configuration and using the same reasoning, eventually for every process p and every neighbor q of p, $p.States[q].d$ will be forever equal to $\|q, r\|$. From that point, the next time a non-root p will update its local state, $p.par$ will be definitely fixed to designate a neighbor q such that $p.States[q].d = \|q, r\| = \|p, r\| - 1 = p.d - 1$. Hence, the system eventually reaches a terminal configuration, where variables d and par define a BFS spanning tree rooted at r.

8.3.4 MEMORY REQUIREMENT

The overhead of the translation in terms of memory requirement consists in multiplying the local memory of each process p by a factor of $\delta_p + 1$, where δ_p is the degree of process p. Hence, if the input algorithm A uses bounded local memories, then the solution we obtain in message passing requires bounded local memories too.

For example, for Algorithm BFS, we obtain a memory requirement in $O((\Delta + 1) \times (\log D + \log \Delta))$ bits per process, where D is an upper bound of the network diameter and Δ is the degree of the network.

Notice that, conformly to the explanation given in Section 2.4.2 (page 21), the transformation supports the intuitive idea that the memory requirement in the atomic-state model is a major indicator of the communication footprint of the message passing version of the algorithm, since the proposed transformation consists in the regular transmission of the local state of each process to its neighbors.

Finally, note also that, in some cases, like for Algorithm BFS, the memory requirement can be slightly enhanced. Indeed, the transformation of Algorithm BFS does not require to send the value of the parent pointer since in BFS, the state of a non-root process depends only on the value of the distance variables of its closed neighborhood, while the state of the root is even independent of the states of its neighbors. Hence, the memory requirement of the message passing version of Algorithm BFS can be reduced to $O((\Delta + 1) \times \log D)$ bits per process.

8.3.5   CHILDREN

A shortcoming of Algorithm BFS and its message passing version is that processes do not know their children in the tree. In this case, the spanning tree can be only used to perform bottom-up computation. To allow top-down computation, we must slightly modify the algorithm so that each process also computes the set of its children. To that goal, each process additionally maintains a Boolean array $Children[]$, indexed on $p.\mathcal{N}$. Then, p piggybacks a Boolean value c in each message sent to each neighbor q. The value c indicates whether $p.par = q$. At each reception of a message from q, $Children[q]$ is set to c. Hence, after the stabilization, the set of children in the tree of every process p is $\{q \in p.\mathcal{N} : Children[q] = true\}$. The overhead in space of this modification is only δ_p bits per process p.

8.3.6   LIMIT

Some silent algorithms written in the atomic-state model actually use an underlining "dynamic" algorithm during the convergence. This latter is eventually stopped after legitimacy is reached. For example, several existing silent algorithms in the atomic-state model, such as [DDL19], are actually silent algorithms for synchronous systems that are brought to asynchronous systems using a self-stabilizing unison algorithm (following the ideas of the *cross-over* composition [BGJ01]). The synchronization mechanisms implemented by a unison algorithm cannot be (at least straightforwardly) brought to message passing using the method of Delaët et al. [DDT06]. Hence, not all silent algorithms can be brought (straightforwardly) to message passing using this method. Up until now, the class of specifications that can be handled using the method of Delaët et al. [DDT06] has not been yet characterized.

8.4   SELF-STABILIZATION ASSUMING BOUNDED-CAPACITY LINKS

We consider now message passing systems equipped with asynchronous fair lossy FIFO links of bounded capacity. Let $C_{\max}$ be a bound on the capacity of all links, i.e., each link can contain at most $C_{\max}$ messages in either directions. Moreover, we assume that any sending through an already full link necessarily fails.

Before going into details, we underline that the solutions presented here are really close to the solutions for unbounded capacity links. Basically, in one case, we use bounded counters with modular increments, while in the other case, we use unbounded counters (actually, integer variables) with standard increments.

8.4.1 MESSAGE PASSING VERSION OF THE TOKEN RING ALGORITHM OF DIJKSTRA

In [Var00], Varghese introduced the principle of *counter flushing* to, in particular, bring solutions from the atomic-state model to the message passing model. He first described a message passing version of the Dijkstra token ring algorithm (studied in Chapter 6). Recall that the network is assumed to be a rooted oriented ring $p_0, \ldots, p_{n-1}$ with $n \geq 3$. Each process p_x has two neighbors: its predecessor p_{x-1} and its successor p_{x+1} (subscripts are understood modulo n). Moreover, p_0 is the root. In the local algorithm of p_x (for every $x \in \{0, \ldots, n-1\}$), we denote the local label designating the predecessor p_{x-1} (resp. the successor p_{x+1}) of p_x by $p_x.Pred$ (resp. $p_x.Succ$).

Following the atomic-state version of the algorithm, each process p_x maintains a single variable $p_x.v$ whose domain is $\{0, \ldots, K_R - 1\}$, where K_R is a strictly positive integer whose value will be discussed later. Moreover, the value of $p_x.v$ should be computed according to the value of $p_{x-1}.v$. Thus, to prevent deadlock, each process p_x uses a timer to regularly (1) send the current value of $p_x.v$ to $p_x.Succ$, and (2) try to receive a message from $p_x.Pred$. Upon receiving a message containing value *val* from $p_x.Pred$, a process p_x updates its local state like in the atomic-state version:

- if p_x is the root (i.e., $x = 0$) and $p_x.v = val$, then $p_x.v$ is incremented modulo K_R, i.e., $p_x.v \leftarrow (p_x.v + 1) \bmod K_R$;

- if p_x is a non-root process (i.e., $x \neq 0$) and $p_x.v \neq val$, then p_x adopts the received value, i.e., $p_x.v \leftarrow val$;

- otherwise, the state of p_x is not modified.

Recall that the main application of token passing is mutual exclusion. To achieve here mutual exclusion once the system has converged, the critical section code should be executed right before an actual local state modification.

Regardless the model in which it is written, the correctness of the algorithm lies of the fact that the domain of each variable $p_x.v$ should be at least as greater as the number of values present in a configuration. In the atomic-state model, such values exist only at the processes, hence the algorithm stabilizes provided that $K_R \geq n$, where n is the number of processes. Now, in message passing, values may also be present in the links. Here, we only need to consider links from predecessors to successors (since counterclockwise links are simply ignored). Hence, overall K_R should be at least greater than or equal to $n \cdot (1 + C_{\max})$ since there is one value per process and n processes as well as at most $C_{\max}$ values per clockwise link and n clockwise links.

In more detail, the fairness of links and processes guarantees that the root p_0 increments its counter $p_0.v$ infinitely often. Hence, the system eventually reaches a configuration in which the value of $p_0.v$ does not exist anywhere else (neither at any other process, nor in a clockwise link). From that point, this fresh value propagates through the ring "flushing" old values and eventually the system reaches a particular configuration where all values in the ring (i.e., at the processes and in the links) are identical, i.e., the root holds the unique token. From that point, every configuration is legitimate in the following sense: let $v_0, v_1, \ldots$ be the values present (both at the processes and in the links) in the configuration ordered clockwise; there is at most one $i > 0$ such that $v_{i-1} \neq v_i$. This latter property guarantees the uniqueness of the token.

8.4.2   DATA-LINK PROTOCOL

The goal of a data-link protocol is to provide to an application layer two high-level primitives, SEND and RECEIVE, allowing to manage a directed link (s, r) in such a way that calls to SEND and RECEIVE (try to) respect all the properties of the reliable FIFO communication, i.e., no creation, no duplication, no loss, and FIFO order despite the link (s, r) is fair lossy. These two primitives require the sending of maybe several messages because of message losses. Consequently, a mechanism should be implemented to discard duplicates. Such a mechanism is inspired from the alternating bit protocol [Lyn68], yet using more than two values.

The data-link protocol between a sender s and a receiver r consists essentially in applying the token ring protocol on the circuit s, r, s, where s is the root.

Precisely, each of the two processes, s and r, has a variable v whose domain is $\{0, \ldots, K_D - 1\}$ with $K_D \geq 2 \cdot (C_{\max} + 1)$ (according to the ring solution).

The sender s regularly sends a data message containing both the data to transmit d and the sequence number $s.v$ to the receiver r. The receiver r regularly transmits an acknowledgment message tagged with its sequence number $r.v$.

Calls to the primitive SEND are sequentialized: the next call SEND(d) can be initiated only after the completion of the previous one, i.e., after the sender s receives an acknowledgment tagged with a value v equal to $s.v$. In this case, s increments $s.v$ modulo K_D, and starts the transmission of d with that new sequence value.

Upon receiving a data message from s, the receiver r first checks if the sequence value v in the message is different from $r.v$. If it is the case, then it delivers the data d in the message to the application layer by calling RECEIVE(d). Otherwise, the message is simply discarded. In either case, it refreshes $r.v$ by setting $r.v$ to v, which will be its new sequence value for its acknowledgment messages.

According to the ring solution, the data-link algorithm converges to a set of legitimate configurations where every legitimate configuration γ satisfies the following requirement: let $v_0, v_1, \ldots$ be the word formed by the value of $s.v$, followed by the sequence values of the messages in transit in (s, r) (from the latest to the oldest messages), the value of $r.v$, and the sequence values of the messages in transit in (r, s); there is at most one $i > 0$ such that $v_{i-1} \neq v_i$.

From such a configuration, the SEND and RECEIVE primitives no more loss or duplicate data, moreover they respect the FIFO order. Nevertheless, we may have a last data creation, i.e., a non-sent data delivered to the application layer. However, if such a creation occurs, it necessarily occurs first at the receiver before any other data delivery.

Finally, notice that, to the best of our knowledge, all existing self-stabilizing data-link algorithms actually achieve nothing but this latter weakened specification. Following the impossibility results proposed by Dubois et al. in [DDPT11], we conjecture that this slight weakening of the original specification is actually necessary.[5]

8.4.3 FROM ATOMIC-STATE TO MESSAGE PASSING MODEL

As previously explained, the main application of the data-link protocol is the conversion of self-stabilizing algorithms written in a locally shared memory model (atomic-state or register model) into the message passing model. We now describe the transformer proposed by Dolev [Dol00]. This transformer assumes a connected rooted network and takes as input an algorithm A written in the atomic-state model which is self-stabilizing under (at least) the central weakly fair daemon. The transformation is made in two steps. First, the input algorithm is brought to the register model (n.b., this model has been briefly presented in Section 1.2.6, page 8), and then from the register to the message passing model. The data-link protocol is involved in the second part of the transformation.

From Atomic-State to Register Model

The overall idea is to emulate the atomic-state model under the central weakly fair daemon in the register model using a self-stabilizing token-based mutual exclusion algorithm in which the critical section (which is performed atomically) consists for the token holder p of reading the states of its neighbors and then executing an enabled action of $A(p)$, if any.

The self-stabilizing token-based mutual exclusion algorithm is obtained in two steps. First, the Dijkstra's token ring algorithm (Chapter 6) is brought into the register model, yet still in a rooted oriented ring. Then, the obtained variant is emulated in a rooted network of arbitrary connected topology.

Bringing the Dijkstra's token ring into the register model is not an issue since each process has to repeatedly and alternately (1) read the variable v of exactly one neighbor, its predecessor, and (2) write its own variable v. However, since the read and write operations do not occur in the same steps, each process p should maintain an additional register in which it stores the last value it reads from its predecessor. Then, the write operation is essentially the same as in the atomic state version: the process compares its variable v to the last value it reads from its predecessor in the ring and updates its variable accordingly. We can remark that running this register version in a ring of n processes corresponds to a sequential execution of the atomic-state version in a ring of $2n$ processes (due to the additional registers). Hence, the self-stabilization is guaranteed for any $K \geq 2n - 1$ by Theorem 6.42, page 83.

The register version of the Dijkstra's token ring is brought to connected rooted networks using a rooted spanning tree. To build a rooted spanning tree, we proceed as in the message

---

[5]The impossibility proof of Dubois et al. in [DDPT11] has been established assuming non-FIFO links, however it seems that it can be adapted to prove our assertion.

passing (see Section 8.3.3), except that we replace message transmissions by read operations. This spanning tree construction is executed concurrently with a slightly modified version of the register version of the Dijkstra's token ring. This latter is run on a *virtual embedded ring* defined by an *Euler tour* of the spanning tree [AS94]; for example, see, the Euler tour in Figure 8.1 and its associated virtual ring in Figure 8.2. Since a spanning tree contains $n - 1$ edges, this virtual ring contains $2n - 2$ nodes. Hence, processes may appear several times in the ring. Actually, each process p appears d_p times where d_p is its degree in the spanning tree. So, each process p should emulate the code of d_p nodes in the ring. In particular, the root process r should emulate one root node code and $d_r - 1$ non-root node codes. Again, the value of K should be chosen according to the size of the virtual ring: the self-stabilization is guaranteed for any $K \geq 4n - 5$. Of course, the effective convergence of the token circulation on the virtual ring starts once the spanning tree construction has stabilized.

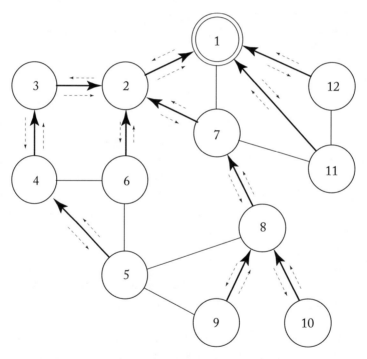

Figure 8.1: Euler tour of a spanning tree given by the dashed arrows. The number inside each node gives its preorder ranking in the tour. An Euler tour actually corresponds to a depth-first search traversal, starting from the root, of the (unoriented) spanning tree.

From Register to Message Passing Model

To emulate the register model in message passing, we should implement self-stabilizing *atomic registers* [VA86], where the values read from the neighbors will be stored. Recall that an atomic

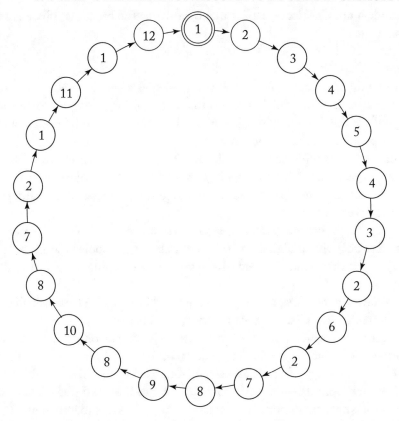

Figure 8.2: The virtual ring defined by the Euler tour proposed in Figure 8.1.

register guarantees that the reads and writes appears to happen at a single point in time. These atomic registers can be simply achieved using the data-link protocol. Each process should (1) regularly send its state to all its neighbors using the high-level primitive SEND and (2) update the local register where it stores the freshest state from its neighbor whenever the high-level primitive RECEIVE delivers a new data for that neighbor.

Actually, the main issue of this latter transformation has been delegated to the data-link protocol.

8.4.4 PROPAGATION OF INFORMATION WITH FEEDBACK (PIF)

Propagation of information with feedback is a crucial tool in distributed computing as it allows to achieve snapshot and reset protocols, for example. It actually consists of two phases: a broadcast phase where a data should be propagated in all the network and delivered (to the application layer) once at each process, and a feedback phase where processes acknowledge the receipt of the data to the initiator of the broadcast. At the end of the feedback phase, a new broadcast can be initiated and so on. Classically, PIF is mono-initiator: the broadcast phase is initiated by a root process.

PIF in Oriented Trees

We first consider oriented trees, i.e., rooted tree topologies where each non-root process p designates its parent (its neighbor which is closest to the root) using a pointer variable, here denoted by $p.par \in p.\mathcal{N}$. In the following, we also denote by r the root and by $Children(p)$ the subset of $p.\mathcal{N}$ designating its children in the tree.[6]

Let's first study a simple non fault-tolerant algorithm for oriented trees. The root r initiates the broadcast phase by (1) initializing to *false* each cell of a Boolean array $r.Ack[]$, indexed on $Children(r)$, and (2) sending a broadcast message (i.e., a message containing the data to broadcast) to all its children.

Upon receiving a broadcast message, an internal process p (i.e., p is neither the root nor a leaf of the tree) also initializes to *false* each cell of its Boolean array $p.Ack[]$, indexed on $Children(p)$, and then sends a broadcast message piggybacking the received data to all its children.

Upon receiving a broadcast message, a leaf process initiates the feedback phase by sending an acknowledgment, also called feedback message, to its parent.

An internal node sends a feedback message to its parent only when its has received a feedback message from each of its children. Similarly, the root decides that the feedback phase is done only after receiving a feedback message from each of its children. To that goal, upon receiving a feedback from its children q, $p.Ack[q]$ is set to true, and if all values of $p.Ack[]$ are true, then either p is an internal node and sends a feedback message to its parent, or p is the root, decides the end of the feedback phase, and is then allowed to initiate a new broadcast phase.

To make this latter algorithm self-stabilizing under the fair lossy link assumption, we follows the ideas of Varghese [Var00], i.e., we roughly adopt the same method as for the ring.

- Each process p maintains a single variable $p.v$ whose domain is $\{0, \ldots, K_T - 1\}$, where K_T is a positive integer whose value will be discussed later.

- Moreover, each non-leaf-process p still maintains a Boolean array $p.Ack[]$, indexed on $Children(p)$.

- Finally, instead of being triggered upon reception, every message (i.e., broadcast and feedback messages) is regularly retransmitted using a timer to prevent deadlock.

  Precisely,

    - every non-leaf process regularly sends broadcast messages to all its children,

    - every leaf process regularly sends a feedback message to its parent, and

---

[6]In a tree, $Children(r) = r.\mathcal{N}$, and $Children(p) = p.\mathcal{N} \setminus \{p.par\}$ for every non-root process p.

– every internal process p regularly sends a feedback message to its parent provided that it believes that its current feedback phase is done, i.e., if $p.Ack[q] = true$, $\forall q \in Children(p)$ (according to the non self-stabilizing solution, this latter condition ensures the eventual synchronization of the feedback phase).

• Moreover, each process p now piggybacks the current value of $p.v$ in each of its messages.

Then, r regularly checks whether $r.Ack[q] = true$, $\forall q \in Children(r)$. If this latter condition is true, then r decides that the previous feedback phase is done and so r can initiate a new broadcast phase: before sending a new broadcast message to each of its children, r first increments $r.v$ modulo K_T and then resets to *false* each cell of $r.Ack[]$.

Then, to ensure that eventually each data is delivered at most once, a non-root process p *accepts* a broadcast message from its parent only if the value *val* inside the message is different from its own variable $p.v$, otherwise the message is simply discarded. If the message is accepted, then p sets $p.v$ to *val* and resets each cell of $p.Ack[]$ to false, if it is not a leaf.

A non-leaf process p *accepts* an acknowledgment message for its child q only if $p.Ack[q] = false$ and the value *val* inside the message is equal to its own variable $p.v$, otherwise the message is simply discarded. If the message is accepted, then p sets $p.Ack[q]$ to *true*.

As for the ring case, convergence is guaranteed if K_T is at least larger than or equal to the number of values present in a configuration: n values at processes and $2 \cdot (n - 1) \cdot C_{\max}$ at links, since each link are used in either direction and there are $n - 1$ links in a tree. So, overall the solution stabilizes if $K_T \geq 2 \cdot (n - 1) \cdot C_{\max} + n$. This latter bound may be refined.

PIF in Connected Rooted Networks

The generalization to arbitrary connected rooted networks roughly consists in composing a silent spanning tree construction (e.g., the one proposed in Section 8.3.1) with the PIF solution for trees. This composition has to be carefully addressed. Indeed, if infinitely many messages of both algorithms are sent through a given link, then the following unfair behavior is possible because the link is fair lossy: in the link, all messages from one algorithm may be lost, while messages from this other are regularly delivered. Of course, this latter behavior causes a starvation in the first algorithm. This problem can be avoid using a simple trick: we encapsulate messages from both algorithms intended to a given link into a single container message. So, the (local) code of each process is re-organized as follows: each process first tries to receive some container messages from each neighbor, then expands the received messages and updates its state in both algorithms accordingly, and finally for each neighbor, prepares a container message (if necessary) and sends it to that neighbor.

Notice also that during the convergence of the spanning tree construction, a non-root process may switch several times between leaf and internal node roles in PIF execution. So, the code should be adapted accordingly. Moreover, the effective convergence of the PIF starts once the spanning tree construction has stabilized.

A drawback of this solution is that the value of K_T depends on both the link capacity and the number of processes. In [LMV16], Levé et al. propose a snap-stabilizing PIF algorithm under the same settings as Varghese. Their solution uses sequence numbers whose domains only depend on the link capacity by considering the problem of the data-link protocol independently of the PIF problem (basically, the data-link is used in their PIF as a black box).

8.4.5   A PIF-BASED UNIVERSAL TRANSFORMER

Although inefficient in terms of memory requirement, the PIF algorithm we have proposed is an important tool, e.g., to establish that the message passing model with bounded local memories and known bound on link capacity has the same expressive power as the message passing model with unbounded local memories and unbounded link capacity. Indeed, as explained before (see Section 8.2), the method proposed by Katz and Perry [KP93] can be seen as a general algorithm that uses a self-stabilizing PIF as black box. Precisely, the transformer of Katz and Perry assumes a rooted and identified network of arbitrary connected topology. This transformer can be implemented using two PIF-based building blocks, respectively achieving a *(global) reset* and a *snapshot* of the network. Using a self-stabilizing PIF, these two latter algorithms are self-stabilizing too.

Reset Algorithm

A reset algorithm aims at reinitializing the system to a pre-defined configuration. Let A be the distributed algorithm running on the system whose variables have to be reset. The reset can be implemented by a PIF where local resets are performed during the broadcast phase. Precisely, the root initiates a reset by suspending its local execution of A, changing its local state in A to a pre-defined one, and broadcasting a "reset" signal in the network. Upon receiving the "reset" signal, the non-initiators also suspend their local execution of A and change their local state in A to a pre-defined one. Each process (including the root) resumes its local execution of A after switching to the feedback phase.

Snapshot Algorithm

The goal of a snapshot algorithm is to gather at the root data which give a *representation* of the configuration of the system. This representation consists of a collection of histories, one per process. Each history consists of a local state and messages received by the process. Here, we assume each process stores its local history into a stack. The computed representation should be consistent to help in verifying the coherence of the system. Let A be the distributed algorithm running on the system. To snapshot A, the overall idea is to flood the network with *markers*. The root initiates a snapshot by becoming marked, resetting its stack to its local state in A (including its own identifier), and sending the *marker* to all its neighbors. Upon receiving the marker, a process becomes marked, resets its stack to its local state in A (including its own identifier), and also sends the marker to all its neighbors, and so on so forth. Then, a marked process pushes on its local stack every A's message received from each given neighbor (together with the incoming channel number) until it receives a marker from that neighbor. Once it has received markers from all its neighbors, its local stack has to be carried to the root.

We must slightly adapt our self-stabilizing PIF algorithm to implement this principle. First, markers are piggybacked in both broadcast and feedback messages, which are transmitted along the tree. However, markers should be also sent to non-tree neighbors. Let $p.NT$ be the non-tree neighbors of any process p. We propose to mark those processes using *token* messages, following the counter flushing technique. That is, every process p also regularly sends to each non-tree neighbor q a token message containing its own counter value $p.v$ and the last counter value of q it received. Each process p maintains two additional arrays:

- a Boolean array $p.Flag[]$, indexed on $p.NT$, such that $p.Flag[q]$ is true if p believes that $q \in p.NT$ has accepted a marker from p, and

- an array $p.Counter[]$, indexed on $p.NT$, where p stores the last value of $q.v$ it receives from $q \in p.NT$.

So, every process p regularly sends a token message containing the pair $(p.v, p.Counter[q])$ to every non-tree neighbor q. Upon participating to a new broadcast phase (i.e., when p accepts a broadcast message), p becomes marked, resets its stack to its local state and all cells of $p.Flag[]$ to false, and starts collecting A's messages. Notice that we enforce any non-root process to be marked only by broadcast messages from its parent. Upon receiving a token message containing (x, y) from q, p executes the following two tasks.

- If $p.v = x$, then p sets $p.Counter[q]$ to x. Notice that if this action actually modifies the value of $p.Counter[q]$, this means that p accepts a token message from q. Moreover, the condition $p.v = x$ is used to enforce each non-root process to accept a broadcast message before accepting any token message from a non-tree neighbor.

- If $p.v = y$, then p switches $p.Flag[q]$ to true meaning that p considers that q has accepted its last marker.

Thus, p collects no A's messages received from its parent. Moreover, p collects A's messages received from q either when $p.Ack[q] = false$ and q is a child, or when $p.v \neq p.Counter[q]$ and q is a non-tree neighbor. Finally, processes have an extra condition to send a feedback message: each process p (even if it is a leaf) should additionally satisfy $p.Counter[q] = p.v \wedge p.Flag[q] = true$, for every $q \in p.NT$ (meaning that markers have been accepted in both sides of any non-tree edge) to be allowed to send a feedback message. Notice that token messages have no impact on the stabilization of the PIF, however they slow down the computation. Finally, once the PIF has stabilized, the size of the domain of the v variables is large enough to guarantee the eventual flushing of the non-tree edges, and so the stabilization of the snapshot algorithm.

To summarize, a marked process collects every A's message received from each given neighbor q until it accepts a marker from that neighbor. Precisely, this marker is stored in a broadcast message if q is its parent, a feedback message if q is one of its children, or a token message if q is a non-tree neighbor. Finally, all local stacks are carried to the root in the feedback messages. Hence, at the completion of the snapshot (i.e., at the end of the feedback phase), the root holds a representation of the configuration of the system.

The Transformer

The transformer is given two inputs: a (non self-stabilizing) algorithm A that withstands the fair loss of messages[7] and a predicate that recognizes representations of its correct configurations. When started from a pre-defined initial (correct) configuration, A is assumed to achieve a suffix-closed specification SP.[8] The transformed version of A, noted T(A), simply consists in composing—following the method discussed at the beginning of Section 8.4.4—A with a self-stabilizing control algorithm which repeatedly

- takes a snapshot of the system,

- tests whether the last snapshot indicates the system was in an incorrect configuration, and

- resets the system to some correct configuration (e.g., the initial configuration of A), if a problem has been detected.

The use of self-stabilizing reset and snapshot algorithms trivially makes the control algorithm self-stabilizing. In turn, this latter ensures that T(A) is self-stabilizing for SP.

Related Work

The transformer of Katz and Perry is clearly inefficient, mainly because it repeatedly performs global snapshots centralized at the root which are costly, in particular, in terms of message length. Actually, its target is not efficiency, rather it is a tool to show the expressiveness of the self-stabilizing property. Several more efficient transformers have been proposed. However, the gain is obtained at the price of reducing the class of problems on which the method applies. For example, in [APVD94], Awerbuch et al. introduce the notion of *local checking*, and propose a method that, given a self-stabilizing global reset algorithm, builds a self-stabilizing solution of any *locally checkable* problem (i.e., a problem where inconsistency can be locally detected) in an identified network. In this work, local checks replace the computation of heavy global snapshots. In [APSV91], authors focus on a restrictive class of locally checkable problems, those that are also *locally correctable*. A problem is locally correctable if the global configuration can be corrected by applying independent corrections on pair of neighboring processes. The proposed solution is fully decentralized since the global snapshot and reset algorithms are replaced by local checking and corrections, which are less expensive in terms of network load.

---

[7]Any non self-stabilizing algorithm for reliable systems can be adapted to withstand fair loss of messages using the alternating bit protocol [Lyn68].

[8]Recall that non suffix-closed specifications cannot be made self-stabilizing; see Section 1.2.5, page 7.

8.5   STABILIZATION TIME IN MESSAGE PASSING

Evaluating time complexity of self-stabilizing algorithms, in particular the stabilization time, in asynchronous message passing systems with fair lossy links is a major issue. Indeed, messages can be lost, and no assumption is made on the drop rate of messages, and on the frequency of message sending. Now, time complexity cannot be bounded under these assumptions, indeed there is no bound on the number of message retransmissions necessary to ensure just one reception.

We now review some proposals to provide time complexity bounds for self-stabilizing algorithms in message passing.

Delaët et al. [DDT06] proposes to compute the time complexity of a solution in more favorable settings. They assume strong synchrony between processors and a reliable communication medium between each two neighbors (no creation, no duplication, and no loss). The reliability can be then interpreted as assuming non-lossy links that are initially empty. The reliability assumption can be justified by the fact that measuring time complexity under unreliable links does not only evaluate the performance of the algorithm, but rather the performance of the whole system, including the network. Following the literature (e.g., [Tel01]), complexity analysis should not be dependent on system-specific parameters. The strong synchrony assumption consists in assuming that all processes progress simultaneously in (global) locked steps. In each step, each process first receives all messages in transit in their incoming links—either no message (if the link is empty), or messages sent during the previous step—then makes local computations, and finally sends new messages to its neighbors. Each step is assumed to last exactly one time unit. Under such settings:

- the BFS algorithm proposed in Section 8.3.3 converges in $O(\mathcal{D})$ time units, where $\mathcal{D}$ is the network diameter;

- the message passing version of the Dijkstra's token ring presented in Section 8.4.1 converges in $O(n)$ time units, where n is the number of processes;

- the PIF for oriented trees given in Section 8.4.4 converges in $O(H)$ time units, where H is the height of the tree;

- the PIF for connected rooted networks exposed in Section 8.4.4 can achieved a stabilization time in $O(\mathcal{D})$ time units using, for example, the BFS algorithm proposed in Section 8.3.3 to build its spanning tree; and

- the data link protocol given in Section 8.4.2 converges in $O(1)$ time units.

Notice that, for the solutions based on the counter flushing technique (the four last bullets), the proof of complexity consists in applying a scheme similar to the round complexity analysis of the Dijkstra's token ring in the atomic-state model (see Section 6.3.2, page 73).

The settings proposed by Delaët et al. [DDT06] may appear to be very restrictive, since the synchronous assumption forbids any interleaving. Varghese [Var00] proposes to evaluate time complexity by considering truly asynchronous executions. Moreover, he assumes that the links may be initially non-empty, but the links are assumed not to lose any message. In this context, if link capacity is assumed to be bounded by C_{max}, then we should additionally assume that the maximum number of messages I_{max} in a link in the initial configuration satisfies $I_{max} < C_{max}$, in order to prevent link congestion. Then, it is assumed that there is no duplication and, except the messages initially in the links, there is no further message creation. Each previous (global) locked step is now replaced by local events of two types: *message transmission*, where a message traverses a link and is delivered at the receiving node, and *process step*, where process tries to receive delivered messages (if any), updates its own state, and finally sends a message to each of its neighbors. Each message transmission and each process step are assumed to last at most one time unit. However, *(*)* locally at each process, whenever an incoming link is not empty, the frequency of message transmission events is assumed to be higher than or equal to the frequency of process step events (n.b., process steps contain message sendings), since otherwise the load of the system will increase infinitely often, and even lead to link congestion when the link capacity is assumed to be bounded.

We should underline that the proposal of Varghese is close to the notion of time units used in classical non fault-tolerant message passing systems [Tel01], where message transmission is assumed to last at most one time unit and process step is assumed to last zero time unit. Roughly speaking, this latter method measures the execution time of an algorithm according to the slowest messages: the execution is normalized in such a way that the longest message delay, i.e., the transmission of the message followed by its processing at the receiving process, becomes one unit of time.

Notice that using the method of Varghese, we surprisingly obtain the same asymptotic bounds as with the first method for our four case studies. However, this is not a general statement. Besides, the Varghese's method has the following shortcoming: the time of a message transmission is constant no matter the network traffic is, i.e., independently of the number of messages in transit at any time. The method proposed in [DDLV17] roughly follows the same lines as Varghese—e.g., asynchronous execution with no message loss, no message creation except the messages initially in the links—yet in at most one time unit we have only the guarantee that an oldest message in each link (if any) has reached its destination. So, we now only underline the differences between the Varghese's approach and that of [DDLV17]. Previous process events are now divided into two types of event: *triggered event* and *recurrent event*. A triggered event is executed immediately at each message delivery. It consists of receiving the message and updating the process local state accordingly. A recurrent event is a task that is regularly executed using a timer (to avoid deadlock if links are initially empty), it consists of updating the process state and then sending a message to each of neighbors. The time to execute any kind of such events is assumed to be zero. However, each process is assumed to perform a recurrent event at least every X units of time, but at most once per time unit. This latter hypothesis replaces hypothesis *(*)*: it ensures that in each directed link, the frequency of message sending is lower than or equal the frequency of message receptions, and so prevents the load of the system to increase infinitely often. Overall, using this approach, the previous asymptotic time complexities are multiplied by the factor $X \cdot I_{max}$ where I_{max} is the maximum number of messages in a link in the initial configuration (this is not a general statement).

To our knowledge, there is no other proposal to evaluate time complexity of self-stabilizing algorithms in message passing. By the way, self-stabilization in message passing, in particular the time complexity of the proposed solutions, is still poorly investigated. For the problem of evaluating the time complexity, the existing methods differ by their level of abstraction, from coarse-grained to fine-grained behavioral description. Fine-grained description involves more system-related parameters, including quantitative measures. A trade-off has to be made for the complexity bound between the accuracy, and its relevance and meaningfulness. Up until now, there is no consensus of the self-stabilizing community on which approach to follow.

Bibliography

[AB93]   Yehuda Afek and Geoffrey M. Brown.   Self-stabilization over unreliable communication media.   *Distributed Computing*, 7(1):27–34, 1993. DOI: 10.1007/bf02278853 9, 22, 110

[AB98]   Yehuda Afek and Anat Bremler-Barr. Self-stabilizing unidirectional network algorithms by power supply. *Chicago Journal of Theoretical Computer Science*, 1998. 110

[ACD⁺17] Karine Altisen, Alain Cournier, Stéphane Devismes, Anaïs Durand, and Franck Petit. Self-stabilizing leader election in polynomial steps. *Information and Computation*, 254:330–366, 2017. DOI: 10.1007/978-3-319-11764-5_8 8, 48

[ADD17]   Karine Altisen, Stéphane Devismes, and Anaïs Durand. Concurrency in snap-stabilizing local resource allocation. *Journal of Parallel and Distributed Computing*, 102:42–56, 2017. DOI: 10.1007/978-3-319-26850-7_6 89

[ADG91]   Anish Arora, Shlomi Dolev, and Mohamed G. Gouda. Maintaining digital clocks in step. *Parallel Processing Letters*, 1:11–18, 1991. DOI: 10.1007/bfb0022438 33, 34, 41, 44

[AKM⁺93] Baruch Awerbuch, Shay Kutten, Yishay Mansour, Boaz Patt-Shamir, and George Varghese. Time optimal self-stabilizing synchronization. In *Proc. of the 25th Annual ACM Symposium on Theory of Computing, (STOC)*, pages 652–661, 1993. DOI: 10.1145/167088.167256 21

[AN05]   Anish Arora and Mikhail Nesterenko. Unifying stabilization and termination in message-passing systems. *Distributed Computing*, 17(3):279–290, 2005. DOI: 10.1007/s00446-004-0111-6 6

[APSV91] Baruch Awerbuch, Boaz Patt-Shamir, and George Varghese. Self-stabilization by local checking and correction (extended abstract). In *Proc. of the 32nd Annual Symposium on Foundations of Computer Science, (SFCS)*, pages 268–277, IEEE Computer Society, 1991. DOI: 10.1109/sfcs.1991.185378 6, 111, 124

[APVD94] Baruch Awerbuch, Boaz Patt-Shamir, George Varghese, and Shlomi Dolev. Self-stabilization by local checking and global reset (extended abstract). In Gerard

Tel and Paul M. B. Vitányi, Eds., *Distributed Algorithms, 8th International Workshop, (WDAG)*, volume 857 of *Lecture Notes in Computer Science*, pages 326–339, Springer, 1994. DOI: 10.1007/bfb0020443 110, 124

[AS85] Bowen Alpern and Fred B. Schneider. Defining liveness. *Information Processing Letters*, 21(4):181–185, 1985. DOI: 10.1016/0020-0190(85)90056-0 14, 15

[AS94] A. Arora and A. Singhai. Fault-tolerant reconfiguration of trees and rings in networks. In *International Conference on Network Protocols*, pages 221–228, October 1994. DOI: 10.1109/icnp.1994.344357 118

[BCT96] Anindya Basu, Bernadette Charron-Bost, and Sam Toueg. Simulating reliable links with unreliable links in the presence of process crashes. In Özalp Babaoglu and Keith Marzullo, Eds., *Distributed Algorithms, 10th International Workshop, (WDAG)*, volume 1151 of *Lecture Notes in Computer Science*, pages 105–122, 1996. DOI: 10.1007/3-540-61769-8_8 108

[BDK08] Olga Brukman, Shlomi Dolev, and Elliot K. Kolodner. A self-stabilizing autonomic recoverer for eventual byzantine software. *Journal of Systems and Software*, 81(12):2315–2327, 2008. Best papers from the 2007 Australian Software Engineering Conference (ASWEC 2007), Melbourne, Australia, April 10–13, 2007. DOI: 10.1016/j.jss.2008.04.028 3

[BDLP08] Christian Boulinier, Ajoy K. Datta, Lawrence L. Larmore, and Franck Petit. Space efficient and time optimal distributed BFS tree construction. *Information Processing Letters*, 108(5):273–278, 2008. DOI: 10.1016/j.ipl.2008.05.016 55

[BDP+10] Samuel Bernard, Stéphane Devismes, Katy Paroux, Maria Potop-Butucaru, and Sébastien Tixeuil. Probabilistic self-stabilizing vertex coloring in unidirectional anonymous networks. In *Proc. of the 11th International Conference on Distributed Computing and Networking (ICDCN)*, volume 5935 of *Lecture Notes in Computer Science*, pages 167–177, Springer, 2010. DOI: 10.1007/978-3-642-11322-2_19 24

[BDPT09] Samuel Bernard, Stéphane Devismes, Maria Gradinariu Potop-Butucaru, and Sébastien Tixeuil. Optimal deterministic self-stabilizing vertex coloring in unidirectional anonymous networks. In *Proc. of the 23rd IEEE International Symposium on Parallel and Distributed Processing (IPDPS)*, pages 1–8, 2009. DOI: 10.1109/ipdps.2009.5161053 29

[BDPV99a] Alain Bui, Ajoy K. Datta, Franck Petit, and Vincent Villain. Optimal PIF in tree networks. In *The 2nd International Meeting on Distributed Data and Structures 2 (WDAS)*, pages 1–16, 1999. 8, 47

[BDPV99b] Alain Bui, Ajoy K. Datta, Franck Petit, and Vincent Villain. Snap-stabilizing PIF algorithm in tree networks without sense of direction. In *The 6th International Colloquium on Structural Information and Communication Complexity Proceedings, (SIROCCO)*, pages 32–46, Carleton University Press, 1999. 22

[BDPV99c] Alain Bui, Ajoy K. Datta, Franck Petit, and Vincent Villain. State-optimal snap-stabilizing PIF in tree networks. In Anish Arora, Ed., *Workshop on Self-stabilizing Systems*, pages 78–85, IEEE Computer Society, 1999. DOI: 10.1109/slfstb.1999.777490 21, 22

[BFJ03] Binh-Minh Bui-Xuan, Afonso Ferreira, and Aubin Jarry. Computing shortest, fastest, and foremost journeys in dynamic networks. *International Journal of Foundations of Computer Science*, 14(2):267–285, 2003. DOI: 10.1142/S0129054103001728 4

[BFP14] Lélia Blin, Pierre Fraigniaud, and Boaz Patt-Shamir. On proof-labeling schemes vs. silent self-stabilizing algorithms. In *The 16th International Symposium on Stabilization, Safety, and Security of Distributed Systems (SSS)*, pages 18–32, Springer LNCS 8756, 2014. DOI: 10.1007/978-3-319-11764-5_2 47, 89

[BGJ01] Joffroy Beauquier, Maria Gradinariu, and Colette Johnen. Cross-over composition—enforcement of fairness under unfair adversary. In *The 5th International Workshop on Self-Stabilizing Systems, (WSS)*, pages 19–34, Springer LNCS 2194, 2001. DOI: 10.1007/3-540-45438-1_2 47, 89, 90, 114

[BGM93] James E. Burns, Mohamed G. Gouda, and Raymond E. Miller. Stabilization and pseudo-stabilization. *Distributed Computing*, 7(1):35–42, 1993. DOI: 10.1007/bf02278854 110

[BK97] Joffroy Beauquier and Synnöve Kekkonen-Moneta. On FTSS-solvable distributed problems. In *Proc. of the 16th Annual ACM Symposium on Principles of Distributed Computing*, page 290, 1997. DOI: 10.1145/259380.259515 6

[Bou07] Christian Boulinier. L'Unisson. Ph.D. thesis, Université de Picardie Jules Vernes, France, 2007. 45

[BPBRT10] Lélia Blin, Maria Potop-Butucaru, Stéphane Rovedakis, and Sébastien Tixeuil. Loop-free super-stabilizing spanning tree construction. In *Proc. of the 12th International Symposium on Stabilization, Safety, and Security of Distributed Systems (SSS)*, pages 50–64, Springer LNCS 6366, 2010. DOI: 10.1007/978-3-642-16023-3_7 8

[BPRT16] Lélia Blin, Maria Potop-Butucaru, Stéphane Rovedakis, and Sébastien Tixeuil. A new self-stabilizing minimum spanning tree construction with loop-free property. *Computing Journal*, 59(2):225–243, 2016. DOI: 10.1093/comjnl/bxv110 47

[BPV04] Christian Boulinier, Franck Petit, and Vincent Villain. When graph theory helps self-stabilization. In *Proc. of the 23rd Annual ACM Symposium on Principles of Distributed Computing (PODC)*, pages 150–159, July 25–28, 2004. DOI: 10.1145/1011767.1011790 45

[BPV08] Christian Boulinier, Franck Petit, and Vincent Villain. Synchronous vs. asynchronous unison. *Algorithmica*, 51(1):61–80, 2008. DOI: 10.1007/s00453-007-9066-x 44

[BT18] Lélia Blin and Sébastien Tixeuil. Compact deterministic self-stabilizing leader election on a ring: the exponential advantage of being talkative. *Distributed Computing*, 31(2):139–166, 2018. DOI: 10.1007/s00446-017-0294-2 8

[CD94] Zeev Collin and Shlomi Dolev. Self-stabilizing depth-first search. *Information Processing Letters*, 49(6):297–301, 1994. DOI: 10.1016/0020-0190(94)90103-1 47, 98

[CDD+16] Alain Cournier, Ajoy K. Datta, Stéphane Devismes, Franck Petit, and Vincent Villain. The expressive power of snap-stabilization. *Theoretical Computer Science*, 626:40–66, 2016. DOI: 10.1016/j.tcs.2016.01.036 5

[CDL+13] Alain Cournier, Swan Dubois, Anissa Lamani, Franck Petit, and Vincent Villain. The snap-stabilizing message forwarding algorithm on tree topologies. *Theoretical Computer Science*, 496:89–112, 2013. DOI: 10.1016/j.tcs.2013.04.012 8

[CDPV02] Alain Cournier, Ajoy K. Datta, Franck Petit, and Vincent Villain. Snap-stabilizing PIF algorithm in arbitrary networks. In *Proc. of the 22nd International Conference on Distributed Computing Systems (ICDCS)*, pages 199–206, 2002. DOI: 10.1109/icdcs.2002.1022257 18

[CDPV06] Alain Cournier, Stéphane Devismes, Franck Petit, and Vincent Villain. Snap-stabilizing depth-first search on arbitrary networks. *The Computer Journal*, 49(3):268–280, 2006. DOI: 10.1007/11516798_20 20

[CDT05] Yu Chen, Ajoy K. Datta, and Sébastien Tixeuil. Stabilizing inter-domain routing in the internet. *Journal of High Speed Networks*, 14(1):21–37, 2005. DOI: 10.1007/3-540-45706-2_104 xiii, 5

[CDV09a] Alain Cournier, Stéphane Devismes, and Vincent Villain. Light enabling snap-stabilization of fundamental protocols. *ACM Transactions on Autonomous and Adaptive Systems*, 4(1):6:1–6:27, 2009. DOI: 10.1145/1462187.1462193 20

[CDV09b] Alain Cournier, Stéphane Devismes, and Vincent Villain. Light enabling snap-stabilization of fundamental protocols. *ACM Transactions on Autonomous and Adaptive Systems*, 4(1), 2009. DOI: 10.1145/1462187.1462193 47

[CFG92] Jean-Michel Couvreur, Nissim Francez, and Mohamed G. Gouda. Asynchronous unison (extended abstract). In *The 12th International Conference on Distributed Computing Systems (ICDCS)*, pages 486–493, IEEE Computer Society, 1992. DOI: 10.1109/ICDCS.1992.235005 8, 33, 45

[CG01] Jorge A. Cobb and Mohamed G. Gouda. Stabilization of routing in directed networks. In *The 5th International Workshop on Self-Stabilizing Systems (WSS)*, pages 51–66, Springer LNCS 2194, Springer Berlin Heidelberg, 2001. DOI: 10.1007/3-540-45438-1_4 8

[Cou09] Alain Cournier. Graphes et algorithmique distribuée stabilisante. Ph.D. thesis, Université de Picardie Jules Verne, Amiens, France, 2009. 20

[CRV11] Alain Cournier, Stephane Rovedakis, and Vincent Villain. The first fully polynomial stabilizing algorithm for BFS tree construction. In *The 15th International Conference on Principles of Distributed Systems (OPODIS)*, pages 159–174, Springer LNCS 7109, 2011. DOI: 10.1007/978-3-642-25873-2_12 47, 60

[CT11] Pranay Chaudhuri and Hussein Thompson. Improved self-stabilizing algorithms for l(2, 1)-labeling tree networks. *Mathematics in Computer Science*, 5(1):27–39, 2011. DOI: 10.1007/s11786-011-0081-6 8

[CYH91] Nian-Shing Chen, Hwey-Pyng Yu, and Shing-Tsaa Huang. A self-stabilizing algorithm for constructing spanning trees. *Information Processing Letters*, 39:147–151, 1991. DOI: 10.1016/0020-0190(91)90111-t 47

[DDF10] Carole Delporte-Gallet, Stéphane Devismes, and Hugues Fauconnier. Stabilizing leader election in partial synchronous systems with crash failures. *Journal of Parallel and Distributed Computing*, 70(1):45–58, 2010. DOI: 10.1016/j.jpdc.2009.09.004 6, 8

[DDH+16] Ajoy K. Datta, Stéphane Devismes, Karel Heurtefeux, Lawrence L. Larmore, and Yvan Rivierre. Competitive self-stabilizing k-clustering. *Theoretical Computer Science*, 626:110–133, 2016. DOI: 10.1016/j.tcs.2016.02.010 8, 47, 89

[DDL19] Ajoy K. Datta, Stéphane Devismes, and Lawrence L. Larmore. A silent self-stabilizing algorithm for the generalized minimal k-dominating set problem. *Theoretical Computer Science*, 753:35–63, 2019. DOI: 10.1016/j.tcs.2018.06.040 54, 114

[DDLV17] Ajoy K. Datta, Stéphane Devismes, Lawrence L. Larmore, and Vincent Villain. Self-stabilizing weak leader election in anonymous trees using constant memory per edge. *Parallel Processing Letters*, 27(2):1–18, 2017. DOI: 10.1142/s0129626417500025 6, 8, 126

[DDPT11] Shlomi Dolev, Swan Dubois, Maria Potop-Butucaru, and Sébastien Tixeuil. Stabilizing data-link over non-fifo channels with optimal fault-resilience. *Information Processing Letters*, 111(18):912–920, 2011. DOI: 10.1016/j.ipl.2011.06.010 111, 117

[DDT06] Sylvie Delaët, Bertrand Ducourthial, and Sébastien Tixeuil. Self-stabilization with r-operators revisited. *Journal of Aerospace Computing, Information, and Communication (JACIC)*, 3(10):498–514, 2006. DOI: 10.1007/11577327_5 6, 111, 114, 125

[DGPV01] Ajoy K. Datta, Shivashankar Gurumurthy, Franck Petit, and Vincent Villain. Self-stabilizing network orientation algorithms in arbitrary rooted networks. *Studia Informatica Universalis*, 1(1):1–22, 2001. DOI: 10.1109/icdcs.2000.840972 8, 47, 89

[DGS99] Shlomi Dolev, Mohamed G. Gouda, and Marco Schneider. Memory requirements for silent stabilization. *Acta Informatica*, 36(6):447–462, 1999. DOI: 10.1007/s002360050180 17, 111

[DH95] Shlomi Dolev and Ted Herman. Superstabilizing protocols for dynamic distributed systems. *Chicago Journal of Theoretical Computer Science*, 1995. DOI: 10.1145/224964.224993 21

[Dij73] Edsger W. Dijkstra. Self-stabilization in spite of distributed control. *Technical Report EWD 391*, University of Texas, 1973. Published in 1982 as *Selected Writings on Computing: A Personal Perspective*, Springer-Verlag, OPT. DOI: 10.1007/978-1-4612-5695-3_7 vi, xiii, 1, 2, 8, 9, 12, 16, 61, 62, 63, 73

[Dij74] Edsger W. Dijkstra. Self-stabilizing systems in spite of distributed control. *Communications of the ACM*, 17(11):643–644, 1974. DOI: 10.1145/361179.361202 xiii, xiv, 1, 8, 9, 12, 16, 61, 62, 63, 73

[DIM93] Shlomi Dolev, Amos Israeli, and Shlomo Moran. Self-stabilization of dynamic systems assuming only Read/Write atomicity. *Distributed Computing*, 7(1):3–16, 1993. DOI: 10.1007/bf02278851 9, 18, 48, 59

[DIM97a] Shlomi Dolev, Amos Israeli, and Shlomo Moran. Resource bounds for self-stabilizing message-driven protocols. *SIAM Journal on Computing*, 26(1):273–290, 1997. DOI: 10.1137/s0097539792235074 110

[DIM97b] Shlomi Dolev, Amos Israeli, and Shlomo Moran.   Uniform dynamic self-stabilizing leader election. *IEEE Transactions on Parallel and Distributed Systems*, 8(4):424–440, 1997. DOI: 10.1007/bfb0022445 7

[DJ16] Stéphane Devismes and Colette Johnen. Silent self-stabilizing BFS tree algorithms revisited. *Journal of Parallel and Distributed Computing*, 97:11–23, 2016. DOI: 10.1016/j.jpdc.2016.06.003 48, 59, 60, 105

[DJPV00] Ajoy K. Datta, Colette Johnen, Franck Petit, and Vincent Villain. Self-stabilizing depth-first token circulation in arbitrary rooted networks. *Distributed Computing*, 13(4):207–218, 2000. DOI: 10.1007/pl00008919 8

[DLD+13] Ajoy K. Datta, Lawrence L. Larmore, Stéphane Devismes, Karel Heurtefeux, and Yvan Rivierre. Self-stabilizing small k-dominating sets. *International Journal of Networking and Computing*, 3(1):116–136, 2013. DOI: 10.15803/ijnc.3.1_116 47, 90

[DMT15] Swan Dubois, Toshimitsu Masuzawa, and Sébastien Tixeuil. Maximum metric spanning tree made byzantine tolerant. *Algorithmica*, 73(1):166–201, 2015. DOI: 10.1007/s00453-014-9913-5 6

[Dol00] Shlomi Dolev. *Self-Stabilization*. MIT Press, 2000. DOI: 10.7551/mitpress/6156.001.0001 xiv, 3, 8, 16, 17, 47, 48, 89, 111, 117

[DOTF94] Ajoy K. Datta, Eugene Outley, Visalakshi Thiagarajan, and Mitchell Flatebo. Stabilization of the x.25 connection management protocol. In *International Conference on Computing and Information (ICCI)*, pages 1637–1654, 1994. xiii, 5

[DPV11a] Stéphane Devismes, Franck Petit, and Vincent Villain.   Autour de l'autostabilisation. 1. techniques généralisant l'approche. *Technique et Science Informatiques*, 30(7):873–894, 2011. DOI: 10.3166/tsi.30.873-894 7

[DPV11b] Stéphane Devismes, Franck Petit, and Vincent Villain.   Autour de l'autostabilisation. 2. techniques spécialisant l'approche. *Technique et Science Informatiques*, 30(7):895–922, 2011. DOI: 10.3166/tsi.30.895-922 21

[DT01] Bertrand Ducourthial and Sébastien Tixeuil. Self-stabilization with r-operators. *Distributed Computing*, 14(3):147–162, 2001. DOI: 10.1007/pl00008934 8

[DT02] Sylvie Delaët and Sébastien Tixeuil. Tolerating transient and intermittent failures. *Journal of Parallel and Distributed Computing*, 62(5):961–981, 2002. DOI: 10.1006/jpdc.2001.1827 6

[DT11] Swan Dubois and Sébastien Tixeuil. A taxonomy of daemons in self-stabilization. *CoRR*, abs/1110.0334, 2011. 9

[DTY15] Stéphane Devismes, Sébastien Tixeuil, and Masafumi Yamashita. Weak vs. self vs. probabilistic stabilization. *International Journal of Foundations of Computer Science*, 26(3):293–320, 2015. DOI: 10.1109/icdcs.2008.12 7, 14

[DY05] Shlomi Dolev and Reuven Yagel. Self-stabilizing operating systems. In *Proc. of the 20th ACM Symposium on Operating Systems Principles, (SOSP)*, pages 1–2, 2005. DOI: 10.1145/1095810.1118590 3

[DY08] Shlomi Dolev and Reuven Yagel. Towards self-stabilizing operating systems. *IEEE Transactions on Software Engineering*, 34(4):564–576, 2008. DOI: 10.1109/TSE.2008.46 3

[FHP05] Wan Fokkink, Jaap-Henk Hoepman, and Jun Pang. A note on k-state self-stabilization in a ring with $k = n$. *Nordic Journal of Computing*, 12(1):18–26, 2005. 61, 63, 65, 72

[FYHY14] Lin Fei, Sun Yong, Ding Hong, and Ren Yizhi. Self stabilizing distributed transactional memory model and algorithms. *Journal of Computer Research and Development*, 51(9):2046, 2014. 47, 89

[GGHP07] Sukumar Ghosh, Arobinda Gupta, Ted Herman, and Sriram V. Pemmaraju. Fault-containing self-stabilizing distributed protocols. *Distributed Computing*, 20(1):53–73, 2007. DOI: 10.1007/s00446-007-0032-2 5, 21

[GH90] Mohamed G. Gouda and Ted Herman. Stabilizing unison. *Information Processing Letters*, 35(4):171–175, 1990. DOI: 10.1016/0020-0190(90)90020-x 8, 33, 44

[GH91] Mohamed G. Gouda and Ted Herman. Adaptive programming. *IEEE Transactions on Software Engineering*, 17(9):911–921, 1991. DOI: 10.1109/32.92911 47, 89

[GHIJ14] Christian Glacet, Nicolas Hanusse, David Ilcinkas, and Colette Johnen. Disconnected components detection and rooted shortest-path tree maintenance in networks. In *The 16th International Symposium on Stabilization, Safety, and Security of Distributed Systems (SSS)*, pages 120–134, Springer LNCS 8736, 2014. DOI: 10.1007/978-3-319-11764-5_9 47

[Gho14] Sukumar Ghosh. *Distributed Systems: An Algorithmic Approach*, 2nd ed., Chapman & Hall/CRC, 2014. DOI: 10.1201/b17224 xiv, 16, 17

[GK93] Sukumar Ghosh and Mehmet Hakan Karaata. A self-stabilizing algorithm for coloring planar graphs. *Distributed Computing*, 7(1):55–59, 1993. DOI: 10.1007/bf02278856 8

[GM91]   Mohamed G. Gouda and Nicholas J. Multari.   Stabilizing communication protocols. *IEEE Transactions on Computers*, 40(4):448–458, 1991. DOI: 10.1109/12.88464 6, 22, 109, 111

[Gou01]   Mohamed G. Gouda. The theory of weak stabilization. In Ajoy K. Datta and Ted Herman, Eds., *Self-Stabilizing Systems, 5th International Workshop, WSS*, volume 2194 of *Lecture Notes in Computer Science*, pages 114–123, Springer, 2001. DOI: 10.1007/3-540-45438-1_8 7

[GT00]   Maria Gradinariu and Sébastien Tixeuil. Self-stabilizing vertex coloration and arbitrary graphs. In Franck Butelle, Ed., *Proc. of the 4th International Conference on Principles of Distributed Systems (OPODIS)*, pages 55–70, Studia Informatica Universalis, Suger, 2000. 24

[HC92]   Shing-Tsaan Huang and Nian-Shing Chen. A self-stabilizing algorithm for constructing breadth-first trees. *Information Processing Letters*, 41(2):109–117, 1992. DOI: 10.1016/0020-0190(92)90264-v 13, 105

[HC93]   Shing-Tsaan Huang and Nian-Shing Chen. Self-stabilizing depth-first token circulation on networks. *Distributed Computing*, 7(1):61–66, 1993. DOI: 10.1007/bf02278857 8, 48

[Her90]   Ted Herman. Probabilistic self-stabilization. *Information Processing Letters*, 35(2):63–67, 1990. DOI: 10.1016/0020-0190(90)90107-9 7

[Her92a]   Ted Herman. Self-stabilization: Ramdomness to reduce space. *Information Processing Letters*, 6:95–98, 1992. DOI: 10.1007/bf02252680 22

[Her92b]   Ted Richard Herman. Adaptivity through distributed convergence. Ph.D. thesis, University of Texas at Austin, 1992. 5, 89, 90, 103, 105, 106

[HHJS03]   Sandra M. Hedetniemi, Stephen T. Hedetniemi, David P. Jacobs, and Pradip K. Srimani. Self-stabilizing algorithms for minimal dominating sets and maximal independent sets. *Computers and Mathematics with Applications*, 46(5):805–811, 2003. DOI: 10.1016/s0898-1221(03)90143-x 47

[HHM00]   John M. Harris, Jeffry L. Hirst, and Michael J. Mossinghoff. *Combinatorics and Graph Theory*. Springer-Verlag New York, 2000. DOI: 10.1007/978-1-4757-4803-1 53

[HL98]   Shing-Tsaan Huang and Tzong-Jye Liu. Four-state stabilizing phase clock for unidirectional rings of odd size. *Information Processing Letters*, 65(6):325–329, 1998. DOI: 10.1016/s0020-0190(98)00006-4 44

[HLH04] Shing-Tsaan Huang, Tzong-Jye Liu, and Su-Shen Hung. Asynchronous phase synchronization in uniform unidirectional rings. *IEEE Transactions on Parallel and Distributed Systems*, 15(4):378–384, 2004. DOI: 10.1109/tpds.2004.1271186 8

[HM08] Markus C. Huebscher and Julie A. McCann. A survey of autonomic computing: Degrees, models, and applications. *ACM Computing Surveys*, 40(3):1–28, 2008. DOI: 10.1145/1380584.1380585 5

[HP92] Debra Hoover and Joseph Poole. A distributed self-stabilizing solution to the dining philosophers problem. *Information Processing Letters*, 41(4):209–213, 1992. DOI: 10.1016/0020-0190(92)90182-u 8

[IJ90] Amos Israeli and Marc Jalfon. Token management schemes and random walks yield self-stabilizing mutual exclusion. In Cynthia Dwork, Ed., *Proc. of the 9th Annual Symposium on Principles of Distributed Computing (PODC)*, pages 119–131, ACM, 1990. DOI: 10.1145/93385.93409 7

[JADT02] Colette Johnen, Luc Onana Alima, Ajoy K. Datta, and Sébastien Tixeuil. Optimal snap-stabilizing neighborhood synchronizer in tree networks. *Parallel Processing Letters*, 12(3–4):327–340, 2002. DOI: 10.1142/s0129626402001026 45

[Joh97] Colette Johnen. Memory efficient, self-stabilizing algorithm to construct BFS spanning trees. In James E. Burns and Hagit Attiya, Eds., *Proc. of the 16th Annual ACM Symposium on Principles of Distributed Computing*, page 288, 1997. DOI: 10.1145/259380.259508 22, 55

[KC99] Mehmet Hakan Karaata and Pranay Chaudhuri. A self-stabilizing algorithm for bridge finding. *Distributed Computing*, 12(1):47–53, 1999. DOI: 10.1007/s004460050055 47, 73, 89

[KC03] Jeffrey O. Kephart and David M. Chess. The vision of autonomic computing. *Computer*, 36(1):41–50, 2003. DOI: 10.1109/mc.2003.1160055 5

[KK07] Sayaka Kamei and Hirotsugu Kakugawa. A self-stabilizing approximation algorithm for the minimum weakly connected dominating set with safe convergence. In *Proc. of the 1st International Workshop on Reliability, Availability, and Security (WRAS)*, pages 57–67, 2007. 47

[KK13] Alex Kravchik and Shay Kutten. Time optimal synchronous self stabilizing spanning tree. In Yehuda Afek, Ed., *Proc. of the 27th International Symposium on Distributed Computing (DISC)*, volume 8205 of *Lecture Notes in Computer Science*, pages 91–105, Springer Berlin Heidelberg, 2013. DOI: 10.1007/978-3-642-41527-2_7 21

[KM06]   Hirotsugu Kakugawa and Toshimitsu Masuzawa.   A self-stabilizing minimal dominating set algorithm with safe convergence. In *The 20th International Parallel and Distributed Processing Symposium (IPDPS)*, page 8, IEEE, 2006. DOI: 10.1109/ipdps.2006.1639550 21, 47

[KP93]   Shmuel Katz and Kenneth J. Perry.   Self-stabilizing extensions for message-passing systems.   *Distributed Computing*, 7(1):17–26, 1993. DOI: 10.1145/93385.93405 7, 8, 110, 122

[KPS99]   Shay Kutten and Boaz Patt-Shamir. Stabilizing time-adaptive protocols. *Theoretical Computer Science*, 220(1):93–111, 1999. DOI: 10.1016/s0304-3975(98)00238-2 5, 21

[KRS99]   Sandeep S. Kulkarni, John M. Rushby, and Natarajan Shankar. A case-study in component-based mechanical verification of fault-tolerant programs. In Anish Arora, Ed., *Workshop on Self-stabilizing Systems*, pages 33–40, IEEE Computer Society, 1999. DOI: 10.1109/slfstb.1999.777484 61, 63

[Lam85]   Leslie Lamport. Solved problems, unsolved problems and non-problems in concurrency. *ACM SIGOPS Operating Systems Review*, 19(4):34–44, 1985. DOI: 10.1145/858336.858339 xiii

[LC10]   Ji-Cherng Lin and Ming-Yi Chiu. A fault-containing self-stabilizing algorithm for 6-coloring planar graphs. *Journal of Information Science and Engineering*, 26(1):163–181, 2010. 8

[LMV16]   Florence Levé, Khaled Mohamed, and Vincent Villain. Snap-stabilizing PIF on arbitrary connected networks in message passing model. In Borzoo Bonakdarpour and Franck Petit, Eds., *Stabilization, Safety, and Security of Distributed Systems— 18th International Symposium, SSS*, volume 10083 of *Lecture Notes in Computer Science*, pages 281–297, 2016. DOI: 10.1007/978-3-319-49259-9_22 110, 122

[Lyn68]   William C. Lynch. Computer systems: Reliable full-duplex file transmission over half-duplex telephone line. *Communications of the ACM*, 11(6):407–410, June 1968. DOI: 10.1145/363347.363366 6, 109, 110, 116, 124

[MK05]   Toshimitsu Masuzawa and Hirotsugu Kakugawa. Self-stabilization in spite of frequent changes of networks: Case study of mutual exclusion on dynamic rings. In Ted Herman and Sébastien Tixeuil, Eds., *Self-Stabilizing Systems, 7th International Symposium, (SSS), Proceedings*, volume 3764 of *Lecture Notes in Computer Science*, pages 183–197, Springer, Barcelona, Spain, October 26–27, 2005. DOI: 10.1007/11577327_13 8

[NA02] Mikhail Nesterenko and Anish Arora. Dining philosophers that tolerate malicious crashes. In *Proc. of the 22nd International Conference on Distributed Computing Systems (ICDCS)*, pages 191–198, IEEE Computer Society, 2002. DOI: 10.1109/icdcs.2002.1022256 6

[NV01] Florent Nolot and Vincent Villain. Universal self-stabilizing phase clock protocol with bounded memory. In *20th IEEE International Performance, Computing, and Communications Conference, (IPCCC)*, pages 228–235, 2001. DOI: 10.1109/ipccc.2001.918656 44

[PV97] Franck Petit and Vincent Villain. Color optimal self-stabilizing depth-first token circulation. In *International Symposium on Parallel Architectures, Algorithms and Networks (ISPAN)*, pages 317–323, IEEE Computer Society, 1997. DOI: 10.1109/ispan.1997.645114 73

[PV99] Franck Petit and Vincent Villain. Time and space optimality of distributed depth-first token circulation algorithms. In Yuri Breitbart, Sajal K. Das, Nicola Santoro, and Peter Widmayer, Eds., *Distributed Data and Structures 2, Records of the 2nd International Meeting (WDAS)*, volume 6 of *Proc. in Informatics*, pages 91–106, Carleton Scientific, 1999. 21, 22

[PV00] Franck Petit and Vincent Villain. Self-stabilizing depth-first token circulation in asynchronous message-passing systems. *Computers and Artificial Intelligence*, 19(5), 2000. 110

[SK87] Morris Sloman and Jeff Kramer. *Distributed Systems and Computer Networks*. Prentice Hall, 1987. 11

[ST07] Abusayeed M. Saifullah and Yung H. Tsin. A self-stabilizing algorithm for 3-edge-connectivity. In Ivan Stojmenovic, Ruppa K. Thulasiram, Laurence T. Yang, Weijia Jia, Minyi Guo, and Rodrigo Fernandes de Mello, Eds., *Parallel and Distributed Processing and Applications*, pages 6–19, Springer Berlin Heidelberg, 2007. DOI: 10.1007/978-3-540-74742-0_4 73

[Tel01] Gerard Tel. *Introduction to Distributed Algorithms*, 2nd ed., Cambridge University Press, 2001. DOI: 10.1017/cbo9781139168724 xiv, 2, 4, 5, 16, 19, 47, 63, 65, 89, 125, 126

[Tix06] Sébastien Tixeuil. *Toward Self-Stabilizing Large-Scale Systems*. Habilitation à diriger des recherches, Université Paris Sud - Paris XI, 2006. 4

[TJH10] Chi-Hung Tzeng, Jehn-Ruey Jiang, and Shing-Tsaan Huang. Size-independent self-stabilizing asynchronous phase synchronization in general graphs. *Journal of Information Science and Engineering*, 26(4):1307–1322, 2010. 45

[TK15]   Volker Turau and Sven Köhler. A distributed algorithm for minimum distance-k domination in trees. *Journal of Graph Algorithms and Applications*, 19(1):223–242, 2015. DOI: 10.7155/jgaa.00354 8, 47

[VA86]   Paul M. B. Vitányi and Baruch Awerbuch. Atomic shared register access by asynchronous hardware (detailed abstract). In *The 27th Annual Symposium on Foundations of Computer Science*, pages 233–243, IEEE Computer Society, Toronto, Canada, October 27–29, 1986. DOI: 10.1109/sfcs.1986.11 118

[Var00]   George Varghese. Self-stabilization by counter flushing. *SIAM Journal on Computing*, 30(2):486–510, 2000. DOI: 10.1137/s009753979732760x 6, 9, 110, 115, 120, 125

[YH15]   Li-Hsing Yen and Jean-Yao Huang. Selfish self-stabilizing approach to maximal independent sets. In *2015 IEEE Trustcom/BigDataSE/ISPA*, vol. 3, pages 9–16, 2015. DOI: 10.1109/trustcom.2015.607 47

[YK96]   Masafumi Yamashita and Tsunehiko Kameda. Computing on anonymous networks: Part I—characterizing the solvable cases. *IEEE Transactions on Parallel and Distributed Systems*, 7(1):69–89, 1996. DOI: 10.1109/71.481599 7

Authors' Biographies

KARINE ALTISEN

Karine Altisen is an associate professor at Grenoble-INP/Ensimag (France). She has been a member of the VERIMAG Laboratory since 1998 and obtained a Ph.D. in 2001. Her current research area combines formal methods and distributed computing. She is interested in theoretical and algorithmic aspects of fault-tolerant distributed systems, including their certification.

STÉPHANE DEVISMES

Stéphane Devismes is an associate professor at Université Grenoble Alpes (France). Since 2008 he has been a member of the Synchronous Team of the VERIMAG Laboratory. He received his Ph.D. in 2006 from the University of Picardie Jules Verne (Amiens, France). In 2007, he spent one year as a post-doctoral fellow at CNRS/Université Paris-Sud. He carries out broad research in theoretical issues of distributed fault-tolerant computing, especially related to self-stabilization.

SWAN DUBOIS

Swan Dubois received a Ph.D. in December 2011 from INRIA and UPMC Sorbonne Universités (Paris, France). He spent one year as a post-doctoral fellow at EPFL (Lausanne, Switzerland). He currently holds an associate professor position at Sorbonne University (formerly University Pierre and Marie Curie). His research domain covers the whole area of fault tolerance in distributed systems with a particular interest for self-stabilization and dynamic systems.

FRANCK PETIT

Franck Petit received a Ph.D. in Computer Science in 1998. He spent more than ten years in the industry in various positions in Computer Science. He joined the University of Picardie Jules Verne (Amiens, France) as an associate professor in 1998. In 2004, he became a professor in the same university. After one year as a visiting researcher with INRIA LIP/ENS Lyon in 2008, he joined Sorbonne University (formerly University Pierre and Marie Curie), with LiP6 in 2009. His research focuses on algorithmic aspects of synchronization, stabilization, and fault tolerance in distributed systems. He also works in the area of networks of mobile robots.

Index

Printed in the United States
by Baker & Taylor Publisher Services